Scrape Your Lists

Scrape Your Lists

Michael Stewart

CONTENTS

| Waypoints: Your Map to the Ride Ahead 1
1 | An Obligation 3
2 | The Checklist Problem 14
3 | List 1: Motorcycle Camping 21
4 | List 2: Balance 25
5 | List 3: The Whole Damn Truth 30
6 | List 4: Annoying 36
7 | List 5: Dark 43
8 | List 6: Observations From The Saddle 47
9 | ◆ Waypoint 2: Throttle & Reflection 53
10 | List 7: Riding Solo 54
11 | List 8: Marta 57
12 | List 9: More Damn Truths 61
13 | List 10: Bakers Vs Bikers 66
14 | List 11: Questions 68
15 | List 12: Proud 73
16 | ◆ Waypoint 3: Throttle and Thought 76
17 | List 13: Fess Up! 77
18 | List 14: You're Wrong! 79

19	List 15: Rebels Without a Pause	82
20	List 16: Rules	85
21	List 17: Food	88
22	List 18: Helmeted Emotions	91
23	◇ Waypoint 4: The Endless Highway	95
24	List 19: Fuel for Thought	96
25	All Lists Must End	100
26	◇ Final Waypoint: Ride Your Route	102
27	◇ Appendix A: Vocabulary You Didn't Know You Need	103
28	Afterword	109

BOOKS BY THE AUTHOR 110

Copyright © 2025 by Michael Stewart
All rights reserved. No part of this book may be reproduced in any manner whatsoever without written permission except in the case of brief quotations embodied in critical articles and reviews.
First Printing, 2023. Revision 2025.

Waypoints: Your Map to the Ride Ahead

Every road trip has its moments: the checklist, the banter, the gas stops, the pullovers, the rants, the near misses, the deep thoughts, and the silly ones. All part of the magic and power of motorcycles.
This book shares many of those moments—mapped along a route loosely guided by waypoints.

If you go off track, no worries. Our waypoints won't badger you. Flip them the biker salute and read as you like.

Got moments of your own? A new waypoint to add?
Share it with us at **Scraping Pegs** on Facebook—we'd love to hear from you.
Either post or message.

◈ Waypoint 1: Kickstand Up

List discrimination, pre-ride chatter, road trip prep tips, road-tested truths, and the rites of passage.

1

An Obligation

"Lists are a form of power." S. Byatt

"So true ... the quote," my Guzzi-riding friend Marta said, pulling off her gloves like she was preparing for battle. "Think about it. Everything of consequence has been meticulously itemized, except for the motorcycle experience. If lists are a form of power, we've been stomped on too long."

"Outcasts," Conrad mumbled.

"Perhaps it's just too elusive to be captured in point form?" Marta asked.

If not for the shitty weather, we'd have been riding.

not talking lists ... the unspoken words, we all thought, but didn't say? ... FOR FUCK'S SAKE!

Instead, we found ourselves huddled indoors at Tony's Deli, involved in a conversation about the power of lists. It was the bleakest weeks of the Dark Season. Only Cam dared to defy our wet, oppressive winter, a season when prudent riders surrender to the embrace of weatherproof, heated, soulless cages.

The truth about motorcycles? They're not always the most sensible choice.

Marta had accepted a contract job involving "multiple items in a single variable" and was falling down a rabbit hole of bullet points. With Marta, all things lead to motorcycles.

"Lists," Tony expounded, "are the engines that propel restaurants. You may eat this, not that. You must pay this amount. It's an orchestra of words harmonized to summon culinary cravings and fuel commerce."

Marta pondered. "They attempt to define and penetrate the very foundation of human existence. The neglect of motorcycles is disheartening." My friend has a knack for connecting things to the world of two wheels. "Tony's right. Menus, recipes, dining and other gastronomic lists, have elevated food while motorcycles wallow in parts lists and spec sheets."

"Motorcycle enthusiasts are too busy exploring to worry about bullet points," Earl offered.

"Reducing biker culture to a series of dots or numbers? I'm skeptical, Marta. Lists are inherently structured and orderly ... they clash with the biker persona."

"Riding is a dance, unshackled by rigid constraints." SQUID Dolores waved her arms as if she were a ballerina.

"Riding is free form, at least in spirit." For me, winter is a time of concession, a season when I embrace the comfort of my wife's EV. "Let's forget about motorcycles ... and lists ... until spring." In life, achieving balance is essential for one's well-being. "Take a break to prevent burnout—you'll find that advice on all self-help lists, Marta."

Marta would not be put off. "According to those who dominate the web, successful people, activities, and products rely on lists extensively. People in powerful positions revere lists. Motorcycles aren't getting on their radar," Marta insisted, revealing a hint of frustration. Perhaps that explains why motorcycles are expected to fall in with cars. Do as they do. No Motorcycle Speed Allowance. No curvy roads. ... We don't have the power of lists ... so the people who run things tell us to get lost."

|5| – AN OBLIGATION

"Brains thrive on organization," Manny agreed, pushing his napkin into a perfect square.

"That explains why we have endless top ten lists of things to do, must-visit places and leisurely pursuits," Den said.

"You won't find motorcycling on any important lists, but does it matter?" Earl asked. "Who cares? Rider's brains must be free thinkers."

"Bucket lists," Manny pointed out.

Marta remained resolute. "Not good enough!"

Conrad shook his head. "We're doing pretty well. Bikers don't need rigid structures. But it is a bit of a kick in the sprockets... being ignored."

"A wound to our rebel hearts." Dolores clutched her chest then flicked her scarf as if auditioning for a daytime soap opera.

"Pure horseshit." Cam's fist pounded the table, causing the coffee mugs to jump. "Motorcycles deserve better." He leaned back, arms crossed, daring anyone to disagree, ready to pound any cager found carrying a list.

"Everyone aspires to have their passion highlighted," SQUID Dolores said. "To be acknowledged and celebrated in the top three."

"Or at least to be included and noticed. Motorcycle don't even make the cut," I agreed, but the group, except for Marta, agreed: attempting to reduce the motorcycle experience to point form would be misguided and foolhardy.

Fueled by righteous indignation, Marta stood. "Shall we bury our heads in our tank bags?"

I played along. "Or conceal ourselves behind our visors?"

"Shove our earplugs in?"

"Drain our oil."

"Miss our turn?"

"Close our top cases?"

"Hey! We seem to be natural listers!" Dolores declared.

Marta pivoted her laptop to display 'The Best Adventure Activities in the World.' She tapped the screen, assuming the air of a coach about to dissect a rival team, then narrowed her eyes like she was about to call a foul. "Look at this!"

The Best Adventure Activities in the World
- Skydiving
- Game Drive in Africa
- Bungee Jumping
- Swimming with Sharks
- Zorbing
- Skiing
- Scuba Diving
- Driving a Car on the Autobahn
- Underwater Scooter Adventure

– AN OBLIGATION

> **WHY MOTORCYCLING DIDN'T MAKE THE LIST**
>
> According to the Bureau of Adventure Pundits, motorcycling doesn't qualify as a real adventure due to:
>
> - Difficult to monetize, even on YouTube
> - No instant replays, half-time shows, or cheerleaders
> - Participants have an image problem
> - No concession stand or upselling opportunities
> - The Motorcycle Lottery reality and no mandatory waivers
> - No fans yelling "woohoo" on command
> - Can't be spun out as a team-building exercise

"Ludicrous!" Conrad slammed the table with a resounding thud, causing a collective frustration to reverberate through the members of our group. "What a load of horseshit!" He jabbed his finger at the list like it had personally insulted him.

"Exactly!" Marta beamed.

And so it began, because we were pissed off.

"Riders ride," Earl said. "We haven't been paying attention to crap like this. We're getting screwed!"

"No doubt golfers, poetry lovers, puzzlers and all the rest are having a good laugh at our expense," Conrad said.

In unison, there was a chorus of "fuck'in Nimrods." (Appendix A: 'Vocabulary' decodes our biker vocabulary.)

"Skydiving? Really?" My head shook in utter disbelief. Skydivers don drab overalls, jump out of planes, and fall straight down. No diverting to check out that neat thing over there. Down they go. Straight down. If they descend at motorcycle speeds, they die. Once down, they're stuck on the ground. Beside a turtle. A dirt bike streaks by to experience JOY further along the trail. Skydivers can't head up the mountain or scoot to Magic Canyon. No vast array of stylish clothing. No adding loud pipes for an extra bit of stimulation. "Skydiving is like riding down a single hill. That's it."

"Zorbing? What the hell is that?"

"Tumbling around inside a giant plastic ball while rolling down a hill."

"In a cage. Out of control. How fuck'in pathetic is that?"

Earl called out to some unsuspecting strangers. "Any of you ever zorbed? Have you heard of zorbing?" Are you planning to go zorbing? The snackers all pretended not to notice. "Not one, but everyone knows about motorcycling. Yet zorbing made the list ... and we didn't."

"Gear heads getting screwed ... the same old story."

Marta had ignited a spark within us, priming us to puncture zorbing balls and then turn our attention to skydiving parachutes.

"Strip away marketing and riding isn't even a footnote on the B or C lists," Marta said, revving us up even more.

Except for Cam, our bikes were tucked away for the winter. Trapped in this limbo, we agreed to Marta's arrangement. We would meet regularly over the winter, with the goal of righting a wrong, but only until the Gotta Go itch moved us on.

"Absolutely no embellishments." Marta listed as her rule #1.

"No baseball-like stats or marketing hoopla."

"No, how-to tips. Lists are not the place to teach riding skills."

– AN OBLIGATION

"Our lists will be honorable."

Cam reminded, "On fine weather days, I may be riding."

We understood—*Gotta Go.*

Taskmaster Marta issued her first assignment: "Think about a list of reasons to ride in the Dark Season, Cameron."

"The rest of us can do a list of 'reasons to park your bike for the winter,'" I suggested.

"Cause your weenies," Cam replied. "Hibernators. Half bikers."

Dolores, who works at a publishing house, interrupted. "What will readers get from this book of lists?"

Marta, armed and ready, tapped her laptop screen with a sense of purpose.

The Top Benefits of Lists

- Relieve stress.
- Help achieve short-term goals.
- Help get things done.
- Provide direction.
- Make long-term goals approachable.
- Bring order to chaos.
- Help remember things.
- Stop procrastination.

She folded the screen down and the banter began.

"Relief from stress? What the fuck?"

"How absurd."

"Can't be serious?"

The correct answer for 'to relieve stress,' is 'ride.' If need be, pull out a list at a rest stop. Debate its merit with a Motorcycle Friend or a Motorcycle Dreamer (Appendix A, Vocabulary). Once you're underway, the stress of discussing the list will dissolve in the wind.

"Imagine a scenario, my friends, where riding is not possible," Marta asked.

"Like for you lot during the Dark Season." Cam waved a hand around our table.

"Or while recuperating from an accident?"

"Or if you throw a rod."

"Jury duty."

"Relatives in town."

"Paint job."

"Jail."

"Family commitment."

"Shipped the wrong part."

"Job deadline."

"Hey!" Dolores was jubilant, bouncing in her seat like a SQUID who had just made a tight turn. "We're listing!"

"I do feel less stressed," Earl mocked.

Marta said, "There is some truth to the 'Top Benefits of Lists,' list, then."

Dolores offered a perspective that was met with frowns. "Motorcycling may be number eleven... just out of the top ten. so it doesn't show on published lists."

Eyes rolled. SQUID Dolores's observations were suspect. "No, Dolores, I'm pretty sure we're not even in the game."

Marta nodded. "Move over skydiving. We're coming for you!"

I chose not to mention it, but I doubt we'll be knocking any activity out of the top ten. Because of our biker persona, outlaws who give society's laws and norms the finger, our fate is to remain list lepers. But from the fringe, Scrape Your Lists will make a statement: fuck you, zorbing, bungee jumping, and sharks! Riders will not remain caged in list purgatory. We have the MAGIC, the JOY, and soon the power of lists.

Filled with a deep sense of camaraderie and determination, we set forth on a mission to infuse the world of itemization with Motorcycle MAGIC.

| 11 | – AN OBLIGATION

***

It was a brutal winter with gloom so frigid we felt the climate changing. All we could do was worry the depleted atmosphere would harm future riding seasons. Will bikers be forced into air-conditioned cages? Are Alaska, the Yukon, and Finland the new touring destinations? Bikers are threatened, but not even a footnote appeared in the plethora of lists generated at the *UN World Climate Change Conferences.*

I was doing my part for the planet, forgoing traveling to Bali for the next summit in favor of driving my wife's EV to Tony's Deli. I attend bike rallies, but they're sensible gatherings. Low carbon footprint. Real products. Skills training. Practical solutions. Riders don't leave with a grand declaration stowed in their tank bags and an extravagant expense claim ready to submit.

The gang would torque, grease, and polish like classic bikers preparing for a show. All, except Cam, agreed to meet twice a week. "Four times, if that's what it takes to finish before riding season."

We turned to Den, an avid reader, for his take spreading the word, to right a wrong. He hesitated before answering. "Kind of like pushing a heavy bike up a hill."

Dolores agreed.

Den scratched his head. "Motorcycle books are always about a trip. Never about lists."

After we restated the power of lists and how motorcycling was getting screwed over by less worthy pursuits, Den became visibly irritated and swore allegiance to our cause. "Count me in! It'll be like writing The Theory of Relativity or 1984. Books that made a difference."

"Only if folks pick our lists up," SQUID Dolores said. "Adventure stories grab attention. Even a mundane trip report is bound to be more interesting than bullet points."

"Any suggestions... to make our list book more compelling?"

"Toss in some photos," I suggested.

"As long as they're relevant," Dolores advised.

As we laughed, Marta chimed in, "In our world, every motorcycle picture tells a story, Dolores. They're all relevant."

LIST ZERO

Before diving into our catalog of overlooked greatness, rest assured, we will not journey down the traps below.

```
LIST 0:
LISTS THAT DIDN'T MAKE THE CUT:

• Top 10 Beginner Mistakes
  (No need to be reminded of the past)
• Best Commuter Bikes Under $5,000
  (Some things are best forgotten)
• Best Motorcycles of All Time
  (We don't want to start a war)
• 5 Ways to Convince Your Partner It's a Good Idea
  (Top secrets will not be disclosed)
• Top 10 Motorcycle Tips from Social Media Influencers
  (Hard pass)
• Trail Breaking Tips
  (We're still practicing)
```

With 'where not to go' agreed, we were ready to turn our attention to defending motorcycles one bullet point at a time. However, engineer Marta insisted we review the current state of motorcycle lists before covering new ground.

2

The Checklist Problem

> *"I ride because I like it. It means something to me. It's my symbol of rebellion—against a stagnant status quo."* Paraphrasing Johnny Cash, talking about why he wore black.

"Even Han Solo and Chewie in Star Wars used them," Conrad said.

"You can't travel through the vast expanse of space without checklists," Earl said.

"Engineers and astronauts swear by them," Marta added. "They're a universal best practice, a lifeline amidst chaos."

We were doing double duty, talking lists and savoring complimentary test kitchen cinnamon rolls still warm and sticky enough to demand finger licking between bullet points. Tony, pacing behind the counter with a cinnamon smear on his apron, was toying with a re-branding idea: attract the morning coffee crowd, swap the word 'Deli' for 'Bistro.' "There'd be a coffee menu and a separate cafe-deli menu. Like Harley offering an adventure bike and BMW a cruiser. Appeal to a broader base. We've done our homework, some competition espionage," Tony admitted.

"Understanding the current state is crucial before forging ahead," Marta, who was helping with the deli transition plan, pointed out. "I've also researched motorcycle lists. Product and gear face-offs dominate. Packing for a road trip is very popular. Experts say the thrill of a trip can sour fast when you realize you forgot to pack essentials, like underwear or a spare spark plug."

"Spark plug?" Conrad raised an eyebrow.

Marta didn't look up. "Padding a checklist is like overfilling your oil."

"How are the buns?" Tony asked.

"Gooey." I grinned, pulling apart a chunk with my fingers. "Just the way I like them."

Marta brought our attention to the list displayed on her laptop, swiveling the screen like a blackjack dealer laying down a losing hand.

Recommended Essentials to Take On Your Bike Trip

- Extra Bike Key
- Jumper Cables
- Tire Repair Kit
- Bungee Cords
- Paper Funnel
- Helmet
- Saddlebags
- Tire Gauge
- Tool kit: Allen wrenches, needle and locking nose pliers, cable ties, additional spark plugs coupled with wires, fuses, screwdrivers, open and closed-end wrenches that are a snug fit for your bike, and light bulbs
- Waterproof Covers for External Storage
- Tail Bags

Following a discussion, Marta compiled her findings.

Our Analysis and Recommendations

A. If the packing checklist appeals to you, consider booking a cruise or a bus tour instead of going on a motorcycle road trip.

B. Pack your credit card—it should be #1. Use it to service your bike so you won't need to bring tools.

C. Phone must be #2. It's your digital Swiss Army knife. Use it to call home for the spare key you forgot to pack, more cash, and to extend your days off.

D. Gas is #3. If you run out of fuel, the stuff you packed won't be going anywhere.

E. Unless you're a mad scientist, forget the paper funnel. Pack needle-nose pliers instead—use them to eat salad out of a bag to maintain good health.

F. If you find the online checklist helpful, leave all the suggested tools at home. You're not capable of fixing anything.

G. Pack a map or update your GPS so you'll know how far up Shit Creek you are when you break down.

H. Instead of packing jumper cables, consider trading your bike for one with kickstart, or replace your ten-year-old battery.

I. You've already got saddlebags and a top box. Need more space? Sign up for a tour with a support van.

J. If you wear a beanie-style half helmet, perform the helmet check.

K. A good list should differentiate riders, like Classic Bikers (CBers), who must carry a complete set of spare parts and a mini fabrication station.

| 17 | - THE CHECKLIST PROBLEM

L. Rather than pack repair stuff, ride with a friend who carries tools and knows how to use them.

M. Pack one of those Good Samaritan Lists. If your bike breaks down, you'll need someone with tools. You left yours at home—because you packed your phone instead, remember?

N. Consider packing thank-you gifts. Give them out to the folks who stopped to help you.

O. Load the user and service manuals on your phone. They'll give you something to read while you're stranded in Shit Creek—right after discovering your warranty expired last week.

P. Substitute a code reader for spark plugs so you won't sound like a SQUID when you call service.

Q. Add duct tape. That way, there'll be one thing in your repair kit you know how to use.

R. Keep the Tire Repair Kit. They provide peace of mind, even if it's outdated and you've never used one.

S. Don't forget headache pills—there isn't a pharmacy in Shit Creek.

T. Consider towing a trailer with a spare bike instead of packing all the crap in the online checklist.

From the same online article, Marta displayed a second list.

Recommended Clothes to Take on Your Trip

• To save room, lay clothing flat, roll tightly, and fit as much as you can in a large Ziploc bag.

• Cram a separate Ziploc with enough underwear and socks to keep you feeling and smelling fresh when you can't make it to a laundromat.

• Given that the temperature and weather are unpredictable, the last thing you need is to be underdressed or overdressed. To avoid resigning yourself to this fate, pack multipurpose garments to save more space in your luggage—such as pants, underwear, and a sweater.

• Visors or hats

• Sunglasses

• Sandals or comfortable walking shoes

• Windbreaker jacket

• Shirts

• Casual socks

• Glasses or contact lenses

• Swimsuit

• Casual or semi-formal wear

<u>Our Analysis and Recommendation:</u> If you found the clothing list informative, ask your mom to pack for you, or better yet, just stay home where all your clothes are.

Lastly Marta displayed:

First Aid Kit Recommendation
- Adhesive tape
- Antibiotic ointment

- Antiseptic wipes
- An antiseptic solution such as hydrogen peroxide
- A splint
- Calamine lotion
- Mouthpiece for administering CPR
- Tweezers
- Anti-inflammatory medication such as ibuprofen
- Alcohol wipes
- Thermometer
- Assorted band-aids
- Blanket
- Elastic bandage
- Plastic non-latex gloves
- Medical scissors
- Sterile gauze pads of different sizes
- Instant disposable cold packs

Our Analysis and Recommendations

A. You've already packed your first aid kit: duct tape, pain pills, a phone to call an ambulance (it will arrive with all the items required), and your credit card to pay for the ambulance and other horrendous medical bills.

B. Ensure your medical insurance policy is paid up.

C. If you packed needle-nose pliers, tweezers are redundant.

D. Spend less time on first aid and more time on situational awareness.

E. Back to the smartphone. Should there be a medical emergency, you'll need your phone to post the crash on social media. Remember, the worst rides make the best stories.

Novice travelers grapple with the age-old dilemma of what to pack and what to leave at home. They often turn to online lists for guidance, but the current state of advice is dismal.

Earl leaned back, wiping cinnamon glaze from his fingertips. "Motorcycle lists are like taking a moped to the track."

"Or a Wing on a trail ride," Conrad said.

Cam chimed in. "An automatic to a hill climb."

Marta rolled her eyes. "A bagger to a naked bike rally."

"Or arriving at a three-wheeler meet on a tidder," I quipped, eliciting a few chuckles.

Marta tapped her keyboard with exaggerated precision. "This is precisely why completing our list project is crucial."

"Any chance of getting another cinnamon roll, Tony?" I asked with a hopeful grin.

Tony sprang into action, performing a couple of impromptu polka steps, his boots squeaking on the deli floor as if in defiance of gravity. "Add Tony's Cinnamon Rolls to the bistro menu, please," he instructed assistant manager, Elena.

Marta closed her laptop screen. "And that's the status quo. Overpacked. Overpolished. Underridden."

We exchanged glances over empty plates and cooling coffee. "Exactly," we agreed. "Game on."

3

List 1: Motorcycle Camping

"All the talk about packing got my dry bag itching," Bull of The Woods Manny said. "The Rockies, I think, next summer."

Motorcycle camping, really?" SQUID Dolores asked, her eyebrows raised in curiosity. "What else?"

"Sleeping beneath a starry sky on the cold, hard ground." I shuddered. "Are you sure?"

Conrad corrected me. "Don't count on starry."

"Bugs and insects. Grizzlies in the mountains," Den added.

"Ashes in your coffee," Earl said.

"Tranquility," Manny countered. "And hiking between stints of throttle therapy. It's the definition of being alive."

Except for SQUID Dolores, the rest of us shared a history of motorcycle camping. We'd logged pleasant memories, including, in hindsight, toughing it out and weathering stormy nights.

Marta lifted her coffee mug like a judge's gavel and then slammed it down on the table with a commanding thud, instantly capturing everyone's attention. "We've got the subject of our first list. Camping is an excellent way to demonstrate the versatility and unrivaled benefits of motorcycles."

"Complementary," Manny agreed, his words a tribute to the synergy between motorcycles and camping.

Dolores looked less than enthusiastic but nodded along with the rest of the gang.

"To start, let's keep it simple." And so we began our quest to right a wrong.

Our Motorcycle Camping List

1. No other travel and accommodation method matches the freedom and independence of motorcycle camping.
2. Motorcycle campers are constantly immersed in nature. Their reward is liberation.
3. Motorcycles can reach unique remote camping spots inaccessible by other vehicles.
4. Camping days are a whirlwind of activity. You're up at the crack of dawn. Dismantle the tent and start loading gear onto the bike. Soon you stop to search for your lost very important tie-down strap. You chart your course by picking out potential campsites down the road. Finally, you're on your way, hoping that the first coffee shop or gas station you come across is open and has a clean indoor washroom available. Throughout the day, your eyes scan for campgrounds. As late afternoon encroaches, a creeping sense of panic settles in—the fear of homelessness. After riding longer than you intended, you secure a spot. Then you unpack, set up camp, prepare a meal or return to the gas station store. You're solo, so you retire early. At 5AM you're wide awake and begin the hunt for your lost sock and, after wrestling into your gear within the confines of your tiny tent, the routine repeats.
5. Unlike the four-wheel version, on two wheels it's difficult to haul all the stuff needed to create the illusion that you're not camping.
6. Be a survivalist—try boondocking! You and your bike don't take up much space and won't be noticed.
7. Camping gear = travel insurance. No room at the inn? No worries—you've got a tent.
8. Wise motorcycle campers pull into motels when the weather is shitty. After all, you've already enjoyed hours out in the elements.

9. At campgrounds, bored lone riders spend hours meticulously cleaning their bikes.
10. Veteran motorcycle campers have fine-tuned mental checklists. Novice campers forget at least one critical item.
11. To lure visitors in, motels flaunt colossal "Welcome" and "Vacancy" signs on main thoroughfares. Unlike motels which want to be found, campsites are elusive—often tucked away at the end of Dog Creek Road or on the outskirts of Rattlesnake Gulch.
12. There is a constant battle between the temptation to wheel into a no-fuss, comfortable motel and the idea of unloading gear and setting up your tent.
13. Timing is critical for lone motorcycle campers. Too early and you're sitting on the ground wondering, What the fuck am I doing here? If you pull in late, you get the last spot—which is always next to the outhouse reeking of cager shit.
14. In Manny's words, there's no bad weather—just improper camping gear.
15. Riding with a camping bag gives you leverage. Use it to bluff your way to a nice room discount.
16. Motorcycle campers prepared to pitch a tent should never jump at a motel owner's first offer.
17. Want to kick-start your day's ride? Wake up in a tent with a stiff back, the flap zipper stuck, and a monster bug in your boot.
18. Why is it the people-in-charge cater to the handicapped, all manner of RVs, walk-ins, and large groups, yet make no effort to accommodate two-wheeled, small-tent, low-impact campers? How about half price for starters?
19. For the occasional motorcycle camper, it's wise to befriend someone well equipped with those small nesting backpacking conveniences.
20. You know you have arrived as a motorcycle camper when you own a tent with a bike port designed to store a full-sized motorcycle.

Marta looked up from her notes. "That's our first truth bomb, folks."

"Not bad," Den said.

Think the world's ready for our truth?" SQUID Dolores asked, stirring her cold coffee as if she were a seasoned rider.

Den shrugged. "Off-motorcycle, there's not a whole lot of truth."

4

List 2: Balance

> *"What the fuck's with recumbent bicycles? Listen, buddy, if you wanna take a nap, lie down. If you wanna ride, buy a fucking motorcycle."* Paraphrasing George Carlin.

It even happens in the food business, falling out of balance. Tony's Deli is a thriving business. Customers are loyal because Tony ventures beyond the ordinary with delicacies like Tony's Battered Pickles, The Cosmic Special, and the Tart of the Month. In contrast, many rival establishments have stagnated. Their lackluster spirit suggested they'd had their fill and no longer cared. Just grinding it out at the It'll Do Cafe.'

Both Tony and Marta understand the need for continual improvement. They possess the spirit of explorers, forever in motion, charting new territories on the culinary map. The transition from "deli" to "bistro" would be a bold step, akin to maneuvering through a culinary minefield. Be careful not to plunge headlong into the deep fryer, Tony!

As in riding, maintaining balance is critical when adding ingredients to transform a business.

How to tell if your Zen's gone sideways.

Signs Your Motorcycle State of Mind May Need Balancing

A. You're using your chin to pull on a riding glove and hit a pothole. Your bike wobbles, but hey, your glove fits perfectly. Smiling, you just ride on.

B. Dodging a near miss into your neighbor's abrupt left turn, their apologetic look has you blushing like a teenager. Shyly, you raise a hand, offering a bashful wave to the adorable culprit.

C. You can't decide which is worse: dealing with the Ass Problem or wasting money on failed mitigation products. Then you buy a breathable beaded cushion with a sheepskin topper.

D. Pulling away from a gas pump, you're serenaded by the lid of your top case as it tap dances up and down. Then a tie-down strap chatters against your rear fender. You reassure yourself, They'll be fine... until the next gas stop.

E. You believe taking the freeway is a great way to save time.

F. It seems like your GPS is set to Road Vomit Mode (Heavy Traffic—see List 6: Words), but rather than turning off, you grind it out where you are.

G. You twist the throttle hard, pull out to pass, and once again are forced to drop back. Because you're out of balance, you immediately prepare for attempt #4.

H. "I'll take the car next time," you reassure yourself, eagerly anticipating the change to four wheels.

I. When you spit, all the liquid flies back in your face. You notice it tastes like spearmint gum.

LIST 2: BALANCE

J. Your signal has been flashing for twenty minutes. You shrug. *I'm good to go for the next right turn.*

K. Once again, you contemplated swapping your motorcycle for a different brand and color, but the gravitational pull of keeping the peace triumphed. There'd be trouble if your spouse noticed your brand new, very expensive toy—the broken dishwasher was the agreed priority. So you traded your old black bike in for a new one that was black and the identical model. Before going home, you drove around to catch some dust and mud puddle splatter.

L. While pondering the gas pump's chocolate bar offer, you inadvertently trigger a gasoline waterfall down your leg, baptizing your brand new boots.

M. A twig is making a clattering sound. You hope it doesn't fall off because it reminds you of your childhood.

N. A wasp gets trapped in your helmet. As the sound of its wings grows fainter you think, *It's probably dying—no need to pull over.* The stinger recovers and launches a kamikaze attack at the apex of the next tight curve.

O. When you took a glove off to scratch, it was snatched away by the wind. You conclude that driving with one bare hand is pretty cool and the way to roll.

P. The sun's intense glare causes you to squint and use your hand as a shield. You have sunglasses but don't stop because you'll be turning east, away from the sun at some point.

Q. As you glance at your GPS, you realize that you've been traveling on the wrong road for 12 miles. In despair, you conclude that your 1000-mile journey is shot to hell, swing around, and head home.

LIST 2: BALANCE   - | 28 |

R. Driving up a hill, you notice that the low tire pressure indicator suddenly came on. You conclude it must be due to altitude, conveniently ignoring the glistening ocean at the bottom of the hill.

S. After a futile five-minute attempt to unlock your top box with the wrong key, you realize you made the same mistake at the previous stop.

T. When your low beam bulb went, you switched to high beam. When your classic biker friend pointed it out, you answered, as if offering advice, "I'm waiting for the high beam to burn out so I can change both at the same time."

U. You fixed a broken signal light stem using duct tape. For the sake of aesthetic symmetry, you place the same fix on the opposite stem.

V. Your birthday? You unwrap a bus pass. You're genuinely thrilled.

W. Rather than washing your bike, you leave it exposed to the rain. But it's parked beneath a tree that constantly oozes sticky brown pollen.

X. Seeing a driving license examiner following a large SQUID on a toy bike leads to uncontrollable laughter.

Cam burst in like a wet dog, dripping puddles, fogging his glasses, and flapping his jacket like wings.
I gave his shoulder a playful nudge. "Take winters off, Cam."
Cam shot back, calling me a "weenie-part-time biker."
Whatever. I didn't argue. It's pointless. I could see Cam was out of balance.
Marta, ever the voice of reason, tapped the table. "Breaks matter, Cameron."

"Absolutely." Cam perked up. "We should fly somewhere warm. Rent bikes. Next meeting, Baja?"

"That might throw off our schedule," Dolores protested.

"We could trailer our bikes down. Work on the way."

Eventually, we all agreed that Cam's Baja idea had merit.

Marta raised an eyebrow. "Shouldn't we compile a rental bike list first?

Cam grinned. "Put it on the to-do list."

Is this is how cults start? I wondered.

5

List 3: The Whole Damn Truth

> *"The Truth is the Truth."* Mahatma Gandhi.

But what is the truth about motorcycles?

"The road teaches truth faster than Mahatma," Marta said. "The power to discern between truth and fiction."

Tony set a test plate of complimentary zesty battered pickles on the biker table. "Have at'er."

"Maybe Mr. Gandhi meant you'll know it when you see it," Dolores suggested.

What I saw was battered pickles, which I'm fond of, but their appearance was jolting because my taste buds were craving fresh gooey doughy cinnamon. "Are they spicy hot?"

"Medium," Tony replied.

Marta quoted Gandhi. "He also said, 'What may appear as truth to one person will often appear as untruth to another.'"

"There are no universal truths," Den declared. "Or very few."

"The wheels are round and they roll." Earl offered a profound truth.

Tony playfully shook a battered pickle at us. "We're simple bikers... not scholars or pundits, but we speak the truth." He threatened us with the pickle and challenged, "Now, take a bite and tell me the truth."

"What about a sweet and sour version?"

"Or extreme dill?"

— LIST 3: THE WHOLE DAMN TRUTH

As Marta slid the pickle tray closer, our conversation took a turn, navigating with the grace of Valentino Rossi, each twist revealing deeper profound truths, draped in the lingering warmth of our beautiful machines.

The Damn Truth

• Motorcycle JOY can't be explained—only ridden.

• Motorcycles are game-changers.

• The Road to Joy will include a few bumps.

• Riders, at their core, are adventurers. They're cut from the same cloth as Sirs Ernest Shackleton and Edmund Hillary, exploring the endless highway with unyielding spirit.

• The blues struggle to keep up at highway speeds. This truth prompted an impromptu chorus of ♪pack up your old tank bag and smile, smile, smile◇.

• The immutable laws of physics reign supreme over motorcycles. Neglect them and misery follows.

• The Highway to Heaven is Heaven. Love the road you're on and ride the paths you're dealt.

• Motorcycles are engineered to respect balance. Riders must respect the design.

• There's MAGIC in the machines—but not for everyone.

• Disengaging situational awareness can cause riders to howl like wounded babies.

- Motorcycle smiles run deep.

- Riding is like playing bingo; you never know when your number will be called.

- Bikers know—indecision is a killer.

- The highway is not boundless. Treasure every moment of your journey.

- Life the Beautiful hangs out on the Road to Joy. Forget the self-help fluff—your throttle knows the way.

- Motorcycle bonds are solid. Human relationships are fragile. When's the last time your bike told you to sleep on the sofa?

- Be careful—motorcycles can be selfish. They're always wanting something: fresh oil, a visit to Service, that neat farkle.

- Motorcycles wait. Kickstands down. "When you want me, I'll be here."

- On two wheels, riders encounter indescribable experiences. All that can be said is: "You had to be there."

- The longer you ride, the less you need to explain.

- Motorbikes can be staunch, comforting friends. It's the Motorcycle Teddy Bear Theory (see Appendix A: Vocabulary).

- "It could have been worse" are words often repeated by riders who walk away from a crash.

- Transport Bikes are strictly business. Any bike can do duty as a Transport Bike.

- LIST 3: THE WHOLE DAMN TRUTH

• The Motorcycle Lottery doesn't care about experience, farkles, or tire pressure.

• "Baby, you can drive my car," the Beatles sang. But not my motorcycles.

• Motorcycles disconnect. Goodbye human jibber-jabber.

• Two-wheelers clear out mental trash—leaving riders with no thoughts and no problems.

• Motorcycles are empowering. Flex your muscles, go for a ride.

• Motorbikes don't like shitty weather.

• Maintaining unwavering vigilance is near impossible. Situational awareness takes catnaps. That's when you spot gravel too late and whisper a prayer to the traction gods.

• The Decision Wall looms (see Appendix A: Vocabulary). Hitting it may end your riding days.

• Adjustments are often required—not in the machines, but within the rider.

• Like decaying lepers in a public pool, motorcycles face vehicle discrimination.

• Not all riders feel they were 'born to be wild.'

• Like Gandalf in *The Lord of the Rings*, classic bikers can do stuff others can't.

• Big bikes aren't fond of parking lot turns.

- Unlike automobiles, motorcycles don't carry spare tires. Riders play tire roulette.

- Small things matter when you're in charge of two-wheelers.

- Motorcycle seats can be JOY killers. It's the Ass Problem (see Appendix A: Vocabulary).

- Bikes, unlike cars, aren't motels. You can't dine, sleep, or have traditional sex while on-motorcycle.

- To see the most critical component, look in the mirror.

- The Gotta Go Itch intensifies the longer you stay put.

- Cagers believe twisties and sweepers result from poor highway engineering.

- Riders don't retire. They recalibrate.

- You never really ride alone. The wind is with you.

- Cagers waste time. Riders stretch it.

- The last ignition of an old bike can break your heart.

- Nothing says freedom like unbuckling your helmet after a 300-mile day.

- Every motorcycle has a soul—some are haunted.

- Some things can't be fixed with duct tape. But many can.

- A good ride is the cure. A great ride is the revelation.

- Motorcycle truths speak loudest—in silence, at a stop, with a buddy.

– LIST 3: THE WHOLE DAMN TRUTH

At this point we were drowning in truth, and collectively yelled, "No more!" But truth doesn't cease to be, just because you've had enough. Continued in List 11: More Damn Truths.

We listened intently, occasionally fiddling with our coffee cups, as Dolores read the points back to us.

Conrad leaned back, arms crossed, as if he were deep in thought.

Den stroked his chin, pondering each truth.

Earl waved a pickle in the air as if conducting an orchestra.

When Dolores concluded, Marta stood, drawing our focus. A hushed anticipation filled the room. She winked. "So what's your verdict. Did we tell the whole damn truth?"

The philosopher spoke: "One may as well try to ride two motorcycles going in opposite directions as record motorcycle truths."

Marta considered Earl's statement for a moment before replying, "Maybe that's the point of our list."

Conrad unfolded his arms and pushed his chair back. "Riding makes you understand why Gandhi left the subject at, 'the truth is the truth.'"

"The wheels are round and they roll," Manny said. "There's nothing more one can say."

"So," Tony began, "what's the verdict on Tony's Spicy Battered Pickles?"

"Not cinnamon rolls," Earl said. "You take the road you're on."

Marta raised her coffee. "It's the ride, not the roll."

6

List 4: Annoying

> "People who think they know everything are a great annoyance to those of us who do."
> Isaac Asimov

Tony, his face alternating between grins and scowls, strolled back from a meeting with his assistant manager. "She can be so damned annoying at times. For the love of god Elena, it's just nutmeg. Ride on!"

"Elena might say the same about you." Marta winked and added. "My dear man."

The conversation shifted gears. "Ever tried parking near the deli lately? Absolute nightmare."

"Drives me nuts... like that Dream Pillow commercial."

"Watching the news is the worst."

"Two flats last season. Still pisses me off."

"The handlebar vibrations on my new bike. Can't get used to it."

"There's always gravel on Humpback asphalt."

"Asphalt period," Cam grumbled.

"And those super bright LEDs running lights? Like staring into the sun," SQUID Dolores offered.

"Then there's Barry Taylor ... look up annoying Blockhead ... and you'll see his picture.'"

"Most cagers."
"The Dark Season."
"Caught in shitty weather."
"Penny Goldberg's sister. She always stays well under the speed limit. Annoying when you gotta wait for her."
"Most SQUIDS and all Blockheads."
"Sore ass."
"No gas station when you're running on fumes."
"Road Vomit."

"Hold that thought," Tony interrupted, standing. "Wanna know what's truly annoying?" He tooted, then did a few polka steps while singing, "Oom-pah-pah. Oom-pah-pah."

Behind the counter, Elena giggled, then shouted, "It's probably the nutmeg you insisted on adding to the cinnamon rolls."

Tony returned to his seat, a satisfied grin on his face.

"There's a seat for every ass," Marta said. "While we're at it, what else grinds your gears?"

Our List of Damn Annoying Motorcycle Challenges

(Or Why You May Need a Beer After Riding)

1. The intermittent and maddening ticking sound you can't pin down.

2. The tiny clips that vanish into unreachable engine crevices.

3. The itch that can't be scratched without pulling over.

4. Stuck in line behind a cager who, upon refueling, abandons their car, chats with a buddy, and then disappears into the convenience store.

5. Having to listen to distorted music you hate blaring from fairing speakers on a nearby bike.

6. The bike leading the way that unnecessarily and abruptly decelerates after overtaking, forcing you to brake hard to squeeze in.

7. The fixer bike that breaks down on every ride. Annoying if it's yours. ... Real annoying if you ride with someone who's bike is always breaking down.

8. SQUIDs stalling and toppling on a hill, forcing you to stop. "Must be something wrong with the engine," they always say.

9. Chaps that reveal too much.

10. Bike snobs who pretend they're not. Aren't we all at least a little?

11. The dude who buys a dirt bike but will only ride on asphalt.

12. Crotchrocket riders with an insatiable need to challenge Transport and It'll Do Bikes to impromptu drag races.

13. The DIY guy who knows it all, but always has a mechanical problem.

14. Riders who help themselves to your very expensive cleaning products.

15. Riders who comb their hair immediately after taking their helmets off.

16. Amateur mechanics who insist on adjusting your bike and mess it up.

17. Riders who fall behind, fail to appear at the designated rendezvous spot, and don't believe in using cell phones while they're 'escaping on their bike.'

18. Being trapped in the middle of a group ride.

19. Labels that say 'water resistant.'

20. Helmet intercoms that don't work when you actually need them. Helmet intercoms that work when you don't need them.

21. The injustice of paying two fees for a pair of bikes that fit in a single parking spot.

22. The tail rider who always misses the traffic light change.

23. Climate change—because nothing says 'buy a car' like riding through apocalyptic wildfires, rain storms, or heat domes.

24. Chicken Little Bikers always expecting the sky to fall.

25. Riders who ask dumb questions at motorcycle presentations. "Learning requires questioning," SQUID Dolores objected to this one.

26. Fixing one bike problem and creating a new one.

27. Slow-moving traffic on a bike requiring movement to cool.

28. In a long line, presenting your ID, credit card, ticket, or passport from the saddle—then dropping one of them.

29. Suiting up for rain, and then it's just a drizzle (SQUID Dolores—"also a blessing").

30. The expensive tight helmet that refuses to adjust to your head shape.

31. Your private mechanic extraordinaire moves, forcing you to pay Service shop rates.

32. Those routine DIY maintenance jobs that require single-use special tools.

33. Nonstandard clips and fasteners.

34. A lengthy ride to a breathtaking destination like the Million Dollar Highway, only to be greeted by the sight of the summit completely shrouded in clouds.

35. A terrific stretch of twisty road plugged by a long caravan of RVs and semis.

36. The frustrating sight of a 'Road Closed' sign when you reach your desired remote destination.

37. You arrive late in a town and there is only one vacant room available. You're with your riding buddy who farts and snores a lot. The room has one bed.

38. Wearing underwear that gives you a wedgy every time you swing your leg over the saddle.

39. Ads that claim mesh jackets can keep you cool.

40. Paying a small fortune to have Dr. Tire confirm 'your valves don't require adjusting.'

41. Engineers who screw up the sidestand length calculations.

42. The inconvenient moment when, immediately after gearing up, nature calls—you must take a dump. Or, in a hurry, you scamper into the woods, barely holding back the floodgates, fumbling with a jammed zipper.

43. The disconcerting sensation of your foot failing to find solid ground as you dismount.

44. Earplugs in. Helmet on. Engine on. A stranger wants to talk to you.

"Number 45—Vehicles parked too close to my bike," Cam shouted, waving his pastry.

❖❖ What Did We Miss? ❖❖
All freedom and wind therapy all the time? Or, has something pissed you off that's not listed?
Please share.
Email us at: beatenstickpress@gmail.com
(We might include it in the next edition—no promises, no prizes, just the righteous satisfaction of righting the motorcycle list travesty).

Tony presented Earl with his prize, a coveted Tart of The Month, for predicting forty-five points.

Annoying. I guessed forty-two.

"Thank you, sir." Earl said, with a triumphant expression on his face, waving his pastry in front of us before taking a bite. "The cure for annoying. Win a free Tart of The Month."

"A beer would take the edge off my annoyance," Manny quipped. "What do you say, Tony? How about applying for a liquor license?"

"Just ride," Cam said. "That's the cure for annoying."

"Or perhaps lose yourself in a good book," SQUID Dolores suggested. "From one of those free little libraries." Using the fingers of both hands, she began tapping her forehead. "If all else fails, try tapping. Top of the head. Or the inner edges or the eyebrow. They say it relieves stress and quiets the mind."

Whatever.

"Tart of The Month then go for a ride," Earl stated.

"Polka at a rest stop." It's Tony's cure for the annoying Ass Problem. Tony took Marta's hand, and they began to dance.

♪Oom-pah-pah! Oom-pah-pah!

That's how it goes!

Oom-pah-pah! Oom-pah-pah!

Ev'ryone knows♦.

Elena leaned on the counter, tapping her fingers and looking irritated. "Sometimes I don't know whether to laugh or cry." Then she turned back to the espresso machine and muttered, "And we're out of nutmeg again."

Dolores burst into an expressive, interpretive dance, waving her arms as if they were wings.

"Dammed annoying," Conrad said.

7

List 5: Dark

> "Riding in the winter separates kids from adults." Cam.

The gang's response? "Or loony from sane," Conrad said. "Sensible from foolhardy? Enthusiasts from potential cult members?"

An oppressive stillness grips the souls of adventurers when the monotonous gray winter sky drapes low over dim mountain passes and waterlogged trails. The urge to ride remains, but you're a captive of the season. Gotta go, but you can't. Below freezing temperatures and dank shadows collude against you.

"Winter, with its biting cold, or summer, searing like a blast furnace, serves as antidotes to excess." This is Marta's belief. "Weather, in its extremes, is a remedy for over indulgence."

"You're implying we should be like hibernating bears, Marta?" I asked.

"No, don't hibernate. Do other things."

Conrad suggested a pragmatic approach: "Why not prepare for the upcoming riding season?"

"Taking a breather doesn't bother me," Manny admitted.

"It weighs on me," Cam confessed. "Short rips, on fine days, during the Dark Season, only whets my appetite for more miles."

"Motorcycles are addictive. Best to go cold turkey for a while, Cam. Park your bike for the winter."

"Step away."

"Recharge your batteries."

"Change your oil."

"How about a Dark Season Activity List?" Dolores proposed. "A set of tasks to keep Cam off his bike and the rest of us somewhat productive."

"Like binge watching the series you missed while you were riding?"

"Hit the gym… get in shape for riding season."

"Read one of those 'How To Ride Like Valentino Rossi' books."

"Sign up for welding class."

"Sleep in. Best dark season activity possible."

"Wax your wife's car."

"Huh?"

"Well, fix the sink then."

"Paint the trim."

There was no shortage of suggestions. We eventually whittled them down to our top twelve.

A Baker's Dozen Dark Season Activities

Pamper your machine.
Buy an expensive miracle detailing kit and use it to clean the underside of your bike.

Become a keyboard warrior.
Watch a few YouTube tutorials—then troll the comment section until spring.

Attempt a new maintenance task.
Then spend the rest of the winter undoing the damage you caused.

Drop farkle gift hints.
Then just go ahead and treat yourself.

Rewatch your favorite motorcycle travel series.
Be thankful you don't have to lug drones, film gear, or calculate charging logistics.

Memorize your owner's manual.
Casually drop obscure torque specs into conversations to impress your friends.

Test your GPS.
Explore one of its lesser-known features just to confirm it's totally useless. No GPS? Drop a few hints (see point #4).

Play tire detective.
Locate and decode your tire's manufacturing date.

Mitigate the Ass Problem.
Channel your inner DIY genius and try to invent a solution.

Sniff test your gear.
Brave the interior of your helmet or jacket like the true rider you are.

Relearn trail braking.
This time, maybe it'll actually click.

Adjust yourself—or your preload.
Drop a few pounds or fiddle with suspension settings and call it even.

Find a better weather app.
One that promises spring is just around the corner and lies convincingly.

Most importantly, once a day, don't forget to: Hug Your Motorcycle Teddy. Or just stare out the window and count down the days until the dark season ends.

8

List 6: Observations From The Saddle

> *"Riding a bike is like an art, something you do because you feel something inside."*
> Valentino Rossi

"This," I gestured at my bun, "is definitely not a cinnamon roll, Tony." Pastries are not always what they appear to be.

"But how's the taste?" Tony inquired, curiosity dancing in his eyes. "Makes you want more coffee, huh?" He was probing his theory that sweet leads to increased coffee orders.

"No, it really grinds my gears because it's misnamed and lacks the honesty I always received from Tony's Deli."

"Ah, but if it bore the name 'sticky bun'…"

"Then I would never order it."

Tony took it in as business feedback. An observation that didn't align well with recent food marketing trends.

The sticky bun topic led Marta to propose our next list: things that fall short of expectations. "Observations less concrete than 'Damn Truths'," she elaborated.

Our Observations

LIST 6: OBSERVATIONS FROM THE SADDLE

- The invisible elixir of life, fresh clean oil, courses through the veins of our machines. You can't always see it on the dipstick, but it doesn't mean it isn't there.

a. Top-heavy bikes and steep hills cause SQUIDS to do the dance of equilibrium. Just before they learn about momentum and the laws of physics.

b. Letting air out of tires won't turn a bagger into an adventure bike. It's like filling a camelback with espresso—lots of caffeine, but it doesn't turn your bike into a coffee shop.

c. The width of the gap between side cases and the object they're attempting to pass through is deceivingly narrower than it appears to be.

d. Traffic cops, the enforcers of rules, aren't swayed by 'no harm done' pleas. To them, a rule is a rule, and excuses sound like 'cry me a river jackass.'

e. Blockheads are their own worst enemy. Check the Appendix, Glossary or spot one wearing flip-flops with their signal light flashing for miles.

f. The best roads start with no destination and end with a story.

g. "Totally makes sense," pianist Cam said, "that Yamaha started as a piano manufacturer." In 1887, the company made a giant leap to manufacturing motorcycles. "Tickling the ivories, like riding, goes beyond technique into the realm of magic."

h. Two-wheel beauty, as seen in the gleam of steel, chrome, and plastic, is truly in the eye of the bike owner.

LIST 6: OBSERVATIONS FROM THE SADDLE

i. To earn your stripes in certain clubs, immerse yourself in the specs and history of their preferred bike brands.

j. There's always a faster, more capable, or prettier bike. "Not if you own a Guzzi," Marta insists.

k. Sooner or later, your helmet will fall and you'll swear *I knew I shouldn't have left it there.*

l. In a testament to human fallibility, every seasoned rider will eventually misjudge a curve. It's a white-knuckle moment that figuratively causes the rider to shit their pants.

m. Tinnitus, the uninvited companion of veteran riders, is a constant reminder—one must suffer for their passion.

n. Being lost in a labyrinth of roads may put you in a better place.

o. The most enjoyable conversations happen with strangers at motorcycle rest stops.

p. Dirt riders can do roads, but the opposite may not be true.

q. You may not see it, but the hole in front of you has a bottom.

r. Adult refreshments taste better after a ride, or as skiers say, après-motorcycling.

s. New tires may save your ass. Old tires can turn your bike into a killer.

t. Although your GPS may occasionally mislead you, it has good intentions.

- u. In the past, almost all females who perished in crashes were passengers sitting behind a male Blockhead. Today, most kill themselves.

- v. It takes a brave person to push a heavy motorbike up a ramp.

- w. Iron Butts receive less respect than their Iron Men or Women counterparts.

- x. If you ride long enough, you'll hear, "Sorry, didn't see you."

- y. Many bikes look goofy. The one you own is always sleek and stylish.

- z. A good bike may outlast your marriage.

- aa. You have two choices: either accept the absurdity of life or ride.

- ab. Nature's grandeur, like lightning and sunsets, is magnified on two wheels.

- ac. Harley engines have the best names—flatheads, panheads, shovelheads, and knuckleheads.

- ad. Climbing on may be the best part of your day.

- ae. If you think you're too old to ride, watch a 75-year-old kickstart a BSA

- af. Your ass remembers long rides better than your GPS.

- ag. The itch in your throttle hand starts days before you ride down Get Out of Dodge Lane.

- ah. The best sound in the world? Your engine starting after a solo stall in the middle of nowhere.

LIST 6: OBSERVATIONS FROM THE SADDLE

ai. Commonly said by senior riders to younger riders, your riding schedule is too aggressive.

aj. Riding in 'shitty weather,' makes you appreciate 'a chance of partially shitty weather.'

ak. X-ray technicians seldom buy motorbikes—they've witnessed many Motorcycle Lottery winners.

al. In the blink of a turn, life can change.

am. Parking Lot Cone School should incorporate lessons on hoping for the best, hunkering down, and grinding it out into their curriculum.

an. Technical skills get you riding. But the soul of the machine? That's the magic carpet under your ass.

ao. People on quests often ride motorbikes.

ap. Motorcycles are mental trash shredders.

aq. Which is more profound, a sermon delivered from a pulpit or a sermon carried on the wind?

ar. Every journey has loose gravel.

as. Riders with the best bikes may have the worst skills.

at. Riding makes overseers, directives, and meetings seem ridiculous.

au. Wind therapy should be included in medical plans.

av. Motorcycles don't ask why. They just ride with you.

aw. You remember your first drop like your first heartbreak—slow motion, inevitable, unforgettable.

ax. Dodge's Tomahawk—a 4-wheel V10 freak haunts the Great Motorcycle Debate. It was labeled a motorcycle, but was it?

Nature always looks better with a motorcycle in it. So does life.

Motorcycles are mirrors—climb on and magnify your life—what needs to be brought into balance and what's still wild in all of us.

Observations were flowing like droplets on a hot exhaust when, suddenly, Manny bolted from his chair. "What's that?" He pointed with a sense of urgency at the spots on Dolores's arm.

Dolores held her left arm up. "Tattoo." A stereotypical biker bad girl design. "Like it?"

"Was the artist six?" Conrad asked, looking at the smudge.

"I'm experiencing biker culture in a personal way. Badass doesn't have to be precise or pretty."

"Doesn't work," Manny said.

"Sort of does," Dolores replied.

"Maybe add a nose ring."

"Streaked hair."

"Skull and crossbones."

"Spike collar."

"A jacket that says 'Biker Mamma.'"

Dolores lowered her arm and said, "Fine, I'll wash it off."

Marta winked.

9
◈ Waypoint 2: Throttle & Reflection

Image. Ego. A lot of learning. A bit of rebellion.

10

List 7: Riding Solo

We'd drunk gallons of coffee and spent countless hours laboring over our noble undertaking. In the past, our moments together had always been interrupted by stretches of two-wheel solitude. Now only Cam had access to the ultimate relief valve. Except for Tony, who had never been a lone rider, we all preferred an occasional solo stint.

Marta was scheduled to go out of town on a business trip. There had been talk of Tony accompanying her, but the demands of the café business extinguished that option. Marta wasn't fazed and charged forward, embracing her impending solitude. "I'll be fine," she assured us. "For me, solitude is a choice to be alone. It's never unwanted isolation or loneliness."

Dolores asked, "Won't you be a teeny bit lonely, Marta?"

"How can I be when I have me for company?" Marta paused. "But I'll miss you lot a tad," she winked, a telltale sign of her love of company. "And Guzzi of course."

"Educate me, please," Dolores asked seriously. "Let's hear your insights on riding solo. I may be ready to give it a try this summer."

"I'm not saying I'm over my fear of it," Dolores added, "but I want to know what I'm missing."

We thought not, but agreed to go around the table to hear what the gang had to say about riding solo.

Earl, the philosopher, started. "We come into the world alone and exit alone. It's in the master plan which is why riding solo is so extraordinary."

Manny went next. "This one's pretty basic. Mike, when you rely on your buddies to carry camping essentials like a pot and coffee, and then go it alone, of course your solo camping experience will be spartan."

"Solo riders don't take orders." Cam said. "There's no telling singles how or where to ride ... or what to think. Tour leaders, instructions, ... the preconceptions and habits of others, hold no sway when you're on your own."

SQUID Dolores listened without commenting, so Conrad went next. "What I like the most about solo is that schedules are not up for debate. Stop and go whenever the hell you like."

Before my turn came, I pondered the exhaustion of large groups and the growing allure peaceful isolation held for me. Since my accident, I grant myself the liberty to choose serenity over annoyance. "When I ride alone, people often look at me as if I've just stepped off a mountain in Tibet or fleeing a crime scene. They're puzzled. I sense they're questioning my sociability. *Does he not have friends ... not even a dog?* They often steer clear, assuming I must possess a surly hermit disposition."

Marta performed an over-the-top wave as she spoke. "Then you smile and wave ... show them your welcoming side. Invite them in to your world."

No, not usually. "Not if I want to be left alone."

Mr. Group Ride, Tony, put forward his view. "Everyone rides alone. Even on group rides, motorcycling is done exclusively inside one's self. I prefer the camaraderie of others while maintaining my independence."

In defense of Tony's stance, Marta offered her perspective. "Two riders who share similar styles and attitudes can be considered a pair of solo riders. Same thing if you're two-up."

"Finding the ideal riding companion for an extended trip must be difficult," Dolores said. "Someone who matches your skill, speed, endurance, and temperament."

"Like Beer Barrel Barry. Rode with him to Richmond a few years ago." Tony shook his head trying to shake a bad memory. "Damn near drove me nuts."

Thinking of something basketball legend Larry Byrd said, I drove to the hoop with my next idea. "Every lone rider is a general, playing their own game."

"Campers think it's sad if you grab a case of beer and stop early, if you're alone," Manny offered.

Den, having returned from the washroom, went next. "Solo riding's got its perks. Like not having to put on pants just to hunt down a greasy diner. Just sprawl in your motel room, chow down on chips, watch sports, and nobody bats an eye. And come morning? If your gut says one more cup of coffee … there's no group standing in the parking lot wondering if you've died on the toilet. Solo means you don't need to apologize for forgetfulness, bowel movements, or being a lazy ass. You ride when you're ready. Bathroom breaks are on your schedule."

"It'd be logical to assume that riding behind a lead bike would offer protection against wildlife. It doesn't." I was following Conrad when Horace the Horrible creamed my GT.

"We may ride solo, but we don't want to be alone forever. I love this quote from Hunter Thompson. 'We are all alone,'" Marta read from her laptop, "born alone, die alone, and—in spite of True Romance magazines—we shall all someday look back on our lives and see that, in spite of our company, we were alone the whole way. I do not say lonely—at least, not all the time—but essentially, and finally, alone.'"

The group fell quiet, nodding as if Marta had quoted scripture, then Conrad jumped in, warding off a Dolores dissertation. "Worse thing for me," Conrad said. "Riding in the middle of a large pack."

"Makes bathroom breaks a performance," I said.

11

List 8: Marta

At Tony's, the gang was seated at our usual table, a huddle of jackets draped over chairs and Cam's helmet placed like a trophy on the windowsill. Dolores was flipping through a riding magazine. Mechanic's art—part grease, part polish—clung to Earl's jacket, hovering like the ghost of a tune-up past. Manny slurped coffee from his chipped rally souvenir mug.

The atmosphere felt off, like when Service tells you they found a big problem while working on what you assumed would be a minor job.

Tony's nonchalant shrug echoed our collective uncertainty, leaving the question hanging in the air: what's our next move?

Marta was on a business trip, poised to leave her employer astounded and her contract expanded. "She sure knows how to charm clients," Tony said. "For an engineer, Marta is remarkably sociable. Always knows how to find the sweet spot."

We'd requested a photo of our friend decked out in her business getup, but received this text instead: 'I'll look forward to seeing a new list or two when I return.'

We thought a tire list might work. Experts on the internet had persuaded Dolores to purchase better ones. "That's why I'm a bit wobbly."

Whatever.

Cam launched into his oft-exaggerated tire explosion tale: "Imagine this—a sudden, ear-splitting boom that nearly knocked me senseless, like a stun gun hit. I was dazed, unsure whether to brake or gas it. Seemed like forever, but quickly I saw brake lights ahead, then tire chunks from a tractor-trailer flying at me."

"If you go down on the freeway, pray you're not flattened like a pancake," Den said knowingly.

"Managed to drive through, dodging black scraps and swerving around a killer metal strip. Lucky a car didn't nail my ass."

"Thank god you had good tires," Dolores noted.

"Following a semi is like tempting fate."

"I go by big rigs as soon as I can."

"Same thing happen to Stu. He was further back when a tire exploded."

There was a thoughtful pause before Dolores gently prodded us. "Tires aren't inspiring much of a list. We need perspective," Dolores sighed. "Marta would have turned this into something about balance, physics, or the cycle of life."

Den nodded. "Exactly. The World According to Marta. A list of Marta-isms."

Each of us had at least one memorable Marta expression in our repertoire.

"The woman claims to be an open book. She won't mind." Tony tapped the office laptop.

Our List of Marta Sayings

On tuning your Motorcycle State of Mind:

- "Let the earth beneath your tires define your days."
- "On-motorcycle, it's not that the world disappears—it just looks better."
- "If you love your motorcycle, sacrifices are easy."
- "When the kickstand's up, the bullshit stops."

- "Convert boredom to awareness," Marta will say when you complain about Nothingness Highway. "Be motorcycle strong. It's a motorcyclefulness opportunity."
- "Ask what can your motorcycle do for you."
- "It'll make sense when you ride or it'll no longer matter."
- "Your motorcycle is your therapist."
- "Autopilot is essential for jets but goes against everything motorcycles stand for."
- "On-motorcycle, it's just you and you realize, there's no better company."
- "The first mile is like finishing an appetizer. Makes me think, what next?"
- "Motorcycle brains are like wheels; they must be well balanced. The soothing motion of Guzzi lulls me back to the womb."
- "When I'm straddling Guzzi, the world is my oyster."
- "Motorcycles don't solve everything. But it doesn't matter as long as you're on one because bikes are anti-bleakness machines."

<u>On grit and reality checks:</u>

- "It's a question every biker will ask. What am I doing riding this horrible chunk of metal? Then you ride another mile."
- "Upset by discrimination? Discover liberation machines." "Never judge a rider by their helmet."
- "Riders who speak the loudest often don't know what they're talking about."
- "Like Mike Tyson says, you have a plan until you're punched in the face."
- "Shitty weather can make you want to car jack the SUV next to you."
- "Convert road rage to defense. Riding away is more effective than walking away."

- About the Ass Problem and her Guzzi: "It's like straddling a log, but I like it."

On riding joy and shared spirit:

- "Riding is like conducting a symphony orchestra."
- "When I wave, I'm sharing a sprinkle of pixie dust."
- "Why are you belly aching? Climb on and bugger off."
- Her pre-ride song: "♪The lights of town are at my back, my heart is full of stars and I'm gonna ride Guzzi again. Oh yes, I'm going to ride Guzzi again◈."

I predicted, "Marta will tell us our list 'makes me sound like a trumpeter.'"

"Or you have me confused with another person."

"Did I say that?" she'll ask.

"Well," Tony said waving his mug, "some of them should be printed motorcycle covers."

When Marta returned, she was in high spirits. Her trip "filled my tank with premium-grade enthusiasm."

I poked Tony. "Another one for the list."

"Or a button," Tony answered.

12

List 9: More Damn Truths

SQUID Dolores held court, her words resounding with authority. "The truth is," she declared emphatically, "readers' eyes will glaze over. Long lists will bore readers. Unlike endless roads, endless bullet points aren't enticing."

"But slicing up truths doesn't sit right," Earl countered. "It distorts the bigger picture."

"It's like a pie," Tony suggested. "Have a slice and enjoy another piece later."

"Like an iron butt ride of twelve hundred miles," Marta added, "you'd split it over days. Same approach for a long list."

"I don't think the truth cares," Conrad said bluntly.

Earl conceded. "As long as it's not hacked or torn."

"We'll tread carefully," Marta promised.

Truths from the Saddle

1. **Motorcyclists remember the flow of the journey more than the destination.**
   Even when Motorcycle Misery joins the ride.
2. **The wheels are round and they roll.**
   Only in motion does the truth emerge.
3. **Balance is a partnership.**
   You and the machine, leaning on each other like old friends.
4. **The Ass Problem cannot be solved.**
   It's a mystery why there aren't franchised Bum Massage Parlors on popular motorcycle roads.
5. **After six hours, you smell like the sum total of the day.**
   Sweet perfume—sweat, fuel, road dust, maybe a hint of pie if you're lucky.
6. **The engine hum in its sweet spot,**
   Is smoother than smooth jazz.
7. **The bike feels different in motion.**
   Only when you stop do, you see what you've been managing.
8. **On-motorcycle, clarity lives.**
   Mind fog kills.
9. **No one has ever had a genuine epiphany inside a group chat.**
   Wind trumps Wi-Fi.
10. **Silence is not awkward on a motorcycle.**
    It's part of the ride. You stop jabbering and listen to the world unfold.
11. **Helmet hair never photographs well.**
    Wave because no one sees it on the road.
12. **The smallest roadside coffee shack has the best espresso.**
    Or maybe the ride made it taste better?
13. **Motorcycle Misery is real.**
    But motorcycle memories forgive, exaggerate, and romanticize.
14. **A single bug, caught just right, can knock sense into you.**
    Or make you a hood ornament on a semi.

15. **Highway hypnosis is real.**
    Curvy roads are the cure.
16. **The bike knows when you're tense.**
    So does your clutch hand.
17. **Motorcycles make ordinary people extraordinary.**
    And the strange fit in.
18. **On-motorcycle, everyone can sing like a diva or devo.**
    Songs composed on-motorcycle don't have to be great.
19. **Caring for a motorcycle is a privilege.**
    Like raising a child, they need attention. Don't skip that maintenance job.
20. **Most deer despise motorcycles.**
    Or they're clueless about road safety.

Let's pull over and stretch. "I hope there's not a test," Manny muttered. The rest of us lined up for the washroom.

Truths From the Rest Stop

1. **Wind therapy requires sacrifices.**
   Unlike playing Halo in the back seat or munching popcorn.
2. **With motorcycles, size matters.**
   But not as much as spirit.
3. **Bikers are a family.**
   They don't always get along.
4. **You don't forget the sweet smell of asphalt after a rain.**
   Unless it starts raining again.
5. **Some truths take thousands of miles to reveal themselves.**
   Others pop up when you stop for pie.
6. **Riding schools are the beginning.**
   There's more to riding than can be taught in a classroom or parking lot.

7. **The smell of chain lube isn't perfume.**
   But it's oddly comforting.
8. **Visors can get foggy.**
   But riding still offers more clarity than most conversations.
9. **Motorcycles are safe harbors.**
   Say whatever you like.
10. **JOY loves sparse traffic.**
    It hates Road Vomit.
11. **Boring often leads to twisting the throttle.**
    Motorcycles don't always stop when you want them to.
12. **Not all bikers look like outlaws.**
    Don't bug the ones that do.
13. **Unlike ships, motorcycles do not carry life rafts.**
    Riders accept the risk of swimming with sharks.
14. **Riding is a journey.**
    Like life condensed in time.
15. **On-motorcycle you must always give a shit.**
    Protective gear is like a knight's armor. It doesn't guarantee your limbs won't be ripped off.
16. **Loud pipes save lives.**
    And make enemies.
17. **How to learn patience?**
    Go on a long road trip, two up with a cager.
18. **Backrests are like engine governors.**
    That's why you never see them at the racetrack.
19. **Riders who haven't gone down hard,**
    Cannot grasp the uneasiness of those who have.
20. **Riders are always in season.**
    Never tune out.
21. **Motorcycles are built to engage.**
    All other vehicles are working toward autonomous drive.
22. **Most road signs should be replaced with:**

LIST 9: MORE DAMN TRUTHS

Or: CAUTION: JOY AHEAD

On the way home, in Dori's EV, I dreaded the forthcoming confession, my admission that I'd failed to plug the car in. *No, you cannot drive over to Dr. Peggy's at this very moment, because I screwed up.*

In the garage, I hooked the car to the grid and commanded, "Charge, baby, charge!" Then I turned to my always understanding motorcycle and offered a figurative embrace before heading upstairs.

"Can Dr. Peggy pick you up?" I asked.

"Why?" Dori wanted to know, her expression puzzled.

"You're almost out of gas." I turned my attention to Bunny, who was rubbing against my leg.

The silence stretched on.

Eventually Dori said, "Really? You always remember to charge your motorcycle battery—but forget the car."

Priorities, Dori. Priorities. That's the truth of the matter.

13

List 10: Bakers Vs Bikers

> *"Anything that gets your blood racing is probably worth doing."* Hunter S. Thompson.

In our cozy corner at Tony's, the conversation flowed like drops of fresh oil falling from a container. Tony, his weathered face wearing a knowing grin, was talking shop. "Baking brings together the creative aspects of art and the logical realities of science, not unlike riding."

Elena's eyes sparkled. "And like riding, it's a whisk-y business."

Tony playfully mimicked drawing revolvers, aiming his fingers at us. "Bake my day."

Elena grinned. "I whisk we were kneading more dough." Their banter was sweet as pie and twice as sticky. "Everyone loves eating. That's why there is a long list of baking expressions."

"Muffin compares to baking,"

"Time to cake it easy."

While Tony and Elena whisked away, the rest of us stewed—until Dolores threw down the oven mitt. "For goodness bakes, there's no reason motorcycling can't play with words just as well as baking."

Marta jumped in. "Wheelie? You think so?"

That got us rolling. We tossed out bikerisms faster than Tony plates pastries.

<u>Motorcycle Sayings to Rival the Best Baking Puns</u>

LIST 10: BAKERS VS BIKERS

- You can lead a NimRod to a bike, but you can't make them ride.
- A little throttle can be a dangerous thing.
- Takes two wheels to tango. Tony corrected, "Polka."
- Leave no road unturned.
- Ride like the wind, but sit out a storm. Cam nodded knowingly.
- Let the bikes out of the garage.
- Dodged a cager. SQUID Dolores nodded as if she'd had a close call.
- Pack up your troubles in your old tank bag and ride, ride, ride.
- Low displacement cutie, shaking her booty.
- Service soon parts bikers from their money. I added, "You can ride that again."
- If the motorcycle fits, buy it.
- Life's short, jump a berm. Cam raised his arm.
- "Climb on and smile, smile, smile."
- "We'll ride across that bridge when we come to it.
- Where there's a trail, there's a way.
- Cop says: "Know why I pulled you over?"
  Biker says: "Because I let you."
  Den scratched his forehead like he didn't get it.

Dolores interrupted. "We're losing focus."

- We've drained the tank.
- Bled the brakes.
- Turned the key.

With that, the table fell into a contented silence.

Eventually, Marta asked with a sly grin, "What do you think, Elena? On par with baking?"

Elena replied, "You lot cake my breath away."

14

List 11: Questions

> *Judge a man by his questions rather than by his answers.*
> Voltaire

"Questions hold more power than answers," SQUID Dolores suggested in a contemplative tone.

Marta, the pragmatist, raised an eyebrow skeptically. "Endless questions without answers? That's an engineer's nightmare, Dolores. It's like chasing solutions you'll never find—futile. Like being a political scientist."

Dolores leaned in, her voice barely above a whisper, "Riding fuels curiosity, you all say. Isn't the quest for knowledge itself enough? Assume nothing. Question everything."

Her words hung in the air, met with blank stares until Conrad said, "If you don't find answers on the road, Dolores, you'll always be a SQUID."

Cam stood. "Going for a rip. Any questions?"

Marta seized the moment. "Why do riders explore, Cam?" She swung her laptop around to display an online list she'd doctored.

Reasons Riders Ask Questions

- To better understand the nature of JOY.
- To resolve route confusion.
- To learn how to fix a mechanical problem.
- To guide motorcycle conversations.
- To gain empathy following a mishap.
- To alter an opinion about riding.
- To learn where a farkle was purchased and for how much.
- To stimulate trip planning ideas.

Marta tilted her laptop screen down and said, "I'm sure you ask questions that go beyond these, Cameron. It won't take long to help us compile a list."

◈ The Zen Questions

- If you drop your motorcycle, causing absolutely no damage and there are no witnesses, did it really drop?
- Do you listen to the news and think, *Folks, you really need to ride?*
- Beyond the rider-machine duality, do things get muddled?
- Have you suffered from a severe case of Motorcyclelessness?
- Do you subscribe to the Motorcycle Teddy Bear Theory?
- Were you Born to Be Wild, with more bravado and luck than skill and ability?
- Has a bike flipped your thinking—suddenly you start giggling?
- Is the song Hallelujah about a motorcycle trip?
- When isn't "ride" the answer?
- Can you imagine the UN full of Motorcycle JOY rather than political science?
- How often do you glance back to confirm your bike is drop-dead gorgeous?

⬥ Nuts & Bolts Questions

- Did you cross the line when you used Peanut's vet money to purchase new tires? Did your excuse—"It was the annual tire sale"—seem pragmatic?
- Have you had the most fun on a less costly machine?
- Is there a perfect windscreen, or is it a myth?
- Do you suspect a marketing executive, not a mechanic, wrote the tool kit spec?
- Does it matter if the loud pipes are on your machine or not?
- Is your machine over-engineered to the degree it makes you complacent? *Point me in the right direction—I'll take it from there, buddy.*
- Are you in a motorcycle rut, wedded to a brand?
- Have you dropped colossal sums of money on a fixer, only to end up doing the smart thing—buying a new bike?

⬥ Riding Questions

- Have you thought—I'd rather not be riding?
- When was the last time you drove too hard and got away with it?
- Do you head for the dugout when the rain arrives?
- Have you been on a road that turned into a racetrack?
- Is your chassis overdue for a tune-up? Are aches, pains, and your riding pants dulling your JOY?
- Do you spin the Motorcycle Roulette wheel when it comes to putting on rain gear?
- Would you sign up for Advanced Rider Blood Circulation Techniques if it were offered (focused on addressing the Ass Problem)?

- Is it advisable to mix old, slow, classic machines with new builds—or is segregation okay?
- Are new models better than old ones—or just more expensive?
- Have you howled out loud because the wind made you feel like a kid?
- Has your motorcycle shown you astonishing sights you otherwise would've missed?

◈ Social Questions

- Are your motorcycle friendships deeper than your car-based ones?
- Thanks to motorcycles, how many strangers have you connected with?
- Do you often think, *Who issued that cager a driver's license?*
- Are you more concerned when your machine makes a strange sound than when your friend does?
- If you ride in formation with large groups, do you feel claustrophobic when you're stuck in the middle?
- Would a pet onboard boost your JOY?
- Is engine hum often more comforting than social chatter?
- Have you admitted to suffering from Motorcycle Narcissism?
- Does your horse carry double? How do you feel about riding two-up?
- Have you switched tribes and had trouble assimilating?

◈ Inspired Questions

- Where is the world's largest art gallery? Daytona? Sturgis? Elefantentreffen? Isle of Man TT?
- When Robbie Maddison soared 107 meters on a motorcycle, was he flying or riding?

- During Emilio Scotto's decade-long, 457,000-mile motorcycle odyssey spanning 279 countries, how much of the time was he lost?
- Why did Dipayan Choudhury ride his motorbike backward for 125.52 miles/202 kilometers?
- Do you boast at parties about the world's longest motorcycle (86 ft) dwarfing the world's longest truck, the Sin City Hustler (32 ft)?

Elena stood patiently behind her boss, waiting for his signature. When there was a pause, she seized the opportunity to ask a question of her own, one that had been on her mind for quite some time. "I have a question," she began, her voice clear and inquisitive.

Tony swung around, his gaze attentive. "Let's hear it, Elena."

With a thoughtful expression, she asked, "Why ride?" Elena's question was simple. But it said everything.

A profound silence settled over the table. Elena's question hung in the air, its simplicity belying its depth. Simply telling a NimRod 'because the wheels are round and they roll' doesn't cut it. But how do you answer?

Marta turned the question around. "Why bake, Elena?"

Elena didn't hesitate. "For sustenance, amongst other things."

"Exactly why we ride, Elena. "For sustenance."

15

List 12: Proud

Close your eyes and envision it—you're standing beside your machine, your heart pounding. Suddenly your name reverberates through the auditorium of the Academy Awards or the Nobel Prize ceremony or the Isle of Man TT winner's circle. It's a moment of unparalleled pride, like many proud motorcycle moments.

A Few of Our Proud Moments

- You roll to a flawless stop at a traffic light—silent victory. You're the Last Boot Down Champion. Hold the applause. Your pride runs deep; you've outgrown the craving for validation.

- Following your lead, the group slows down. Sure enough, a cop was sitting behind the overpass. At the next stop, your buddies swear you're clairvoyant, or maybe a savant.

- Among the gleaming bikes, yours stands out—either for its showroom shine or the thick coat of mud that proves you rode the hardest.

- The day the SQUID label is shed is monumental, a personal triumph etched in the annals of your life's journey.

- Strangers pass by a row of bikes, indifferent—until they stop at yours. That's the one they admire.

- As your mates roll in, you greet them with a sly grin and the question, "What took you so long?" A subtle assertion of your mastery over the road that day.

- When you resisted peer pressure for the first time, rode at your own pace, and experienced a great sense of satisfaction, you were proud to arrive last at the meetup point.

- When your buddies reveal the numbers—you paid 25% less for the same farkle.

- Every time you press start, your engine fires up—that's pride you can hear.

- It's a red-letter day when you can comfortably keep pace with the fast group. No panic braking. No fear of death. Just proud.

I tried to sound serious, but the mischief crept in. "Besides motorcycles, I take immense pride in knowing the world's finest cinnamon bun artisans."

Tony's grin widened. Gesturing for Elena to come closer, he said, "You've got to hear this."

I restated my words, emphasizing their importance. "I was saying you make the greatest cinnamon rolls on the planet."

"Really?" Elena asked. "Even with all that nutmeg?"

I nodded. "I'm proud to know the bakers and eat their rolls."

Den raised his bun. "It's an honour."

Manny interjected, "Got another one for the list. I've decided to have my ashes placed in my helmet. It's all in my will."

LIST 12: PROUD

"Which one?" Conrad asked. "The white or teal one?"

16

◈ Waypoint 3: Throttle and Thought

Emotional gear shifts. Self-tuning. Regrets, joy, and roadside insights.

17

List 13: Fess Up!

According to online experts, the most common motorcycle mistakes are:

- Stalling.
- Forgetting to cancel turn signals.
- Not wearing protective gear.
- Not downshifting before stopping.
- Dropping your bike.

Dolores admitted to four out of five—but firmly added, "I always wear full gear."

"Those aren't blunders?" Conrad teased. "They're classic SQUID moves."

Seeing Dolores' confusion, we each confessed to committing at least one blunder.

Blunders We're Willing to Admit
- The ill-fated purchase of a used machine that turned into a bottomless money pit.
- That weird farkle that looked brilliant online.
- Buying based purely on specs.
- The sidestand not fully flipped down, triggering a frantic save attempt.

- The ever-growing glove pile—they felt right at the time.
- That sinking feeling as your brand-new helmet rolls off your seat onto concrete.
- "Follow me—I know the way." Miles later, turns out you didn't.
- Meticulously careful—then you spill the container of small fasteners and lose the irreplaceable one.
- Everyone's in sleek, coordinated gear. You look like you rolled out of a picked-over garage sale.
- When a NimRod nearly t-boned you, you couldn't find the horn or use your gloved finger.
- Your first and last attempt at a rattle-can paint job. Picasso would weep.

When we were finished, Dolores said, "Got one. Leaving your bike on its sidestand because you fear the centerstand."

"Not a blunder," I replied. "More a way of avoiding a blunder."

18

List 14: You're Wrong!

Intense eye contact locked them in a silent standoff—jaws clenched, brows furrowed, like rivals at a high-stakes motorcycle rodeo.

"Respect the ratio," Tony said flatly. He wasn't talking about gears.

"Purity," Elena shot back. "But they're your buns." With that, she pivoted and stomped off. Peacemaker Marta followed.

Tony shook his head, watching Elena go with equal parts exasperation and admiration. "That woman," he muttered. "If she rode, it'd definitely be a crotchety naked bike."

The dynamics between an employee and their boss can be challenging, each providing the other with reasons to ride.

I couldn't help but interject. "There's nutmeg in this?" I asked, pointing at my cinnamon roll.

Tony nodded. "Elena will live with it, but I'll never hear the end of it."

When Marta returned, she asked, "What else do we disagree about?"

The showdown shifted from a culinary-spice clash to motorbike disagreements.

Our list of Debatable Points:

- "Ideal riding weather? More mindset than meteorology? You're kidding," we answered Manny, recalling days of wringing out socks and dodging heatstroke.

- Farkles aren't investments—unless you're like Earl and insisted his custom seat paid for itself by not buying sore ass pills.
- Outgrowing your motorcycle jacket doesn't mean you need to buy a new larger bike. Tony strongly disagreed.
- Touring bikes don't need running lights that could be searchlights. "Unless you're lost in Bolivia," Cam said.
- Loud pipes are primarily a safety tool. Most placed Motorcycle Narcissism ahead of safety.
- "Lost on a motorcycle? Impossible," we joked, until Dolores said she got lost riding to Marta's.
- Life is not a race—until you meet a bike, you know you can beat.
- Bikes are life-affirming. "Not for Oddballs," Den pointed out. "They're on a different path."
- 'Trios are lovely—motorbike, rider and passenger.' We'd all stopped riding two up.
- Divided highways: relaxing sanctuaries or soul-sucking slabs of boredom? Verdict: mixed.
- Old men don't ride dirt bikes. "Wait and see," was Cam's answer.
- Bikes never criticize or condemn. "I once owned a Cranky Bike," Earl said.
- Motorcycle JOY is like the love of a devoted dog. Tony's not a dog lover.
- It's hard to find JOY if you're in poor shape. 'Just packs good pills," Den said.
- Broken bones change how you ride. "Depends which bones and how many," I argued.
- Riding can cure things medical science can't. "Let's not promote voodoo science," Dolores lectured.

Just as nutmeg stirs up bakery battles, bikers don't always see eye to eye. It explains why there are so many brands, styles, and opinions. And why your riding buddies are always just a gear click away from a good argument.

| 81 | - LIST 14: YOU'RE WRONG!

19

List 15: Rebels Without a Pause

"Why fit in when you were born to stand out?" Dr. Seuss.

OR

Salute this!

Cam's uniqueness shone brightly in our midst because he rode during the Dark Season, a rebel amongst outlaws. The rest of us blended in. For instance, I drove my wife's electric car to our meetings, and it disappeared seamlessly into the winter landscape. When I parked it, I never glanced back over my shoulder. *It's just a car. No reason to draw attention to it.* I was just one of the crowd.

Cam, with his broad shoulders and confident stride, always looked like a knight in shining armor when he strolled into Tony's. Clad in an all-weather suit, he was ready for winter warfare, but we all wondered, 'who's he kidding?'

On this day I greeted him, "Welcome, Cam of the North."

Cam simply nodded in response. "Weenies."

"Lone wolf," Conrad said.

The teasing continued. "Missed the boat for Shackleton's Antarctic run?"

"Don't you feel a little out of place, Cam?" SQUID Dolores asked.

"Like a burger at Tony's."

"A Templar knight in a mosque."

"A diesel at a Tesla rally."

"A frogman in the desert."

"Good for you for not running with the herd," Marta raised her coffee mug, breaking the cycle of jest. "It's refreshing." And so the stage was set for the morning's list.

How Not to Fit In

- Ride a bike with extreme ape hangers (except in southern California).
- Park your 63cc tiddler between two brutes.
- Ride an automatic with Ninja H2s and Hayabusas.
- Take your Indian to the HOG gathering.
- Ride a BMW R18 cruiser to track day dressed in racing leathers.
- Show your 10-year-old machine at a classic bike show.
- Bring a Japanese adventure bike on a GS ride.

LIST 15: REBELS WITHOUT A PAUSE   — | 84 |

- Wear chaps to the trail ride.
- Bring your Spyder to the poker run and win the top prize money.
- Install a hitch when your buddies are converting their bikes to café racers.
- Swap tough cases for colored soft saddle bags on your adventure bike.
- Add a weird rattle can highlight to your gas tank.

At least we're not 1%ers," Earl said, referring to outlaw motorcycle club bikers. "No pins, patches, knuckle tattoos, or shady side businesses."

I stood. "Gotta pick up some sour cream for Dori." I walked back to the EV and when I got home, took the garbage out and then walked my dog Pearly. Despite Pearl not having a dog license, we illegally jay walked across Mann Avenue.

Not all bikers are criminals. Most of us carry a smear of rebellion—a quiet defiance woven into the fabric of everyday life. Whether it's riding through winter, jaywalking with an unlicensed dog, or giving the occasional road sign or ordinance the biker salute—it's just how we roll.

Cam never looked back at his parked bike. He didn't need to. It always waited for him like a loyal best friend with frost on its paws.

20

List 16: Rules

> "If you follow all the rules, you miss all the fun."
> Katharine Hepburn.

Regulations weigh on me. But lawmakers insist: "Without our rules, life would be a complete shit show." Politicians themselves don't agree on what constitutes good governance and while I have strong reservations about the quality of their work, I acknowledge that humanity, like sheep, requires herding. This is precisely why lists are so valuable and practical. They maintain order through manageable, digestible points—suggesting rather than imposing. A quality even rebels can appreciate. Lists aren't a big stick. They nudge, not shove. That's why even rebels read them. No flashing red lights. No condescending committee legalese. Just quiet nudges. "The brilliance of lists," Marta says.

Consider how people interpret the Ten Commandments. Nestled within a list, they invite personal judgment and interpretation. Single out a Commandment, and it's a different story. Standing alone, *"Thou shalt not kill"* becomes an afterlife dealbreaker. Most take notice. But nested in a list, it loses much of its gravity. We read between the lines. Justify exceptions.

When we read the Commandments in list form, like 'thou shalt not commit adultery' and 'thou shalt not bear false witness,' we think, *maybe I will, maybe I won't.* It can't be that important. It's not an independent clause. Just part of an ordinary list, along with many other suggestions.

The downtime following my accident gave me a chance to reflect and refine my guidelines. My Motorcycle Riding Rules (MMR), though I loathe to call them 'rules', are intended to keep me out of harm's way. Yes, I used that repugnant word, 'rules.' It bugs me today—I should have used 'Motorcycle Riding Reminders.' My saving grace? They are in list form.

It's not as if I climbed Mount Sinai and saw the light or even the glow of heavenly riding lights in the distance. Nor am I an Isle of Man TT winner or an Iron Butt finisher, so my rules don't even have the clout of a respected endorser. I figuratively carry my rules in my back pocket, tucked out of the way, nudging me to be aware and sensible. Unfortunately, they don't ward off giant stags.

Dolores, still early in her riding journey, is building her own rulebook—one rooted in cones, clutch finesse, and survival.

Things like:
- Practice slow-speed maneuvering.
- Control the clutch with two fingers.
- Learn my brake's limits.
- Read the corners.
- Look where I want to go (And hope the bike agrees.).

It's impossible not to notice, killing and death are repetitive themes in my version. Your mind goes there after an accident. Now I'm working on restoring my state of mind.

Here's a glimpse of my rule list. For the full run down please read *Scraping Pegs, The Truth About Motorcycles.*

My Motorcycle Riding Rules

1. Everyone is Trying to Kill You.
2. Don't Kill Yourself Doing Something Stupid.
3. Ignore Motorcycle Physics, and It Might Kill You.

4. Your Motorcycle May Be Trying to Kill You.
5. Complacency Will Try to Kill You.
6. Your Noggin Is Trying to Save You—Use It.
7. Be Stubborn, But in a Good Way.
8. Your Number May Come Up—Be Ready.
9. Irritants Will Try to Get Your Goat (and your focus).
10. The Multiplier Effect Could Kill You.

◈ Rule #11: No Motorcycle JOY? Do Not Ride! (Consider this an override switch.)

"Not everyone has to climb Mount Everest," Marta says. Don't break #11.

Tony leaned back. "And don't forget Rule #22: No discussing riding rules while riding."

SQUID Dolores added, "Unless you're about to crash."

"Or with a guy who rides a chopper trike," said Earl.

21

List 17: Food

Chewing It Over

"There should be a list of what to eat when riding," Earl proposed. Den looked up from his leftover diet veggie plate. "Rule one: not this." I pointed at my cinnamon roll. "Rule two: this."

"Just like riding, there are plenty of food rules," Tony said.

"Different," Dolores insisted. "What you put in your body should be regulated. It's common sense—not heavy-handed."

"Sure, the board of health matters," Tony continued. "But baking—like riding—is part science, part art. It's about flow." Then, like he was shifting gears mid-thought, Tony stood. "From now on, it's just 'Tony's.' No more 'Deli.' Free to journey wherever good food and coffee take us."

"Bikes are a blend of physics challenges and sales gimmicks." he says. "Menu items are a culinary challenge wrapped in taste buds. Selling a motorbike or an entré is much the same."

"You've arrived," I said, "when your business can just be a name."

"Delis," Tony said, "have become the rat bikes of the food industry—functional, unglamorous, a little rough around the edges."

"Functional but misunderstood?" I asked.

"Not sleek. Not trendy. Get the job done, but customers want bistros and trendy cafes," he replied.

"Certainly not state-of-the art for new age foodies," Marta agreed.

"Over processed animal junk food, vegans might say," Dolores said. "To some, 'Deli' has become as distasteful as the word cager."

"Doesn't matter if you avoid preservatives and use quality ingredients," Tony lamented. "Deli has a negative connotation today."

Manny, working on a winter rat bike project, defended the concept. "I like delis!"

"Time to let go. Appeal to a wider clientele. Coffee connoisseurs with money to burn. Processed meat lovers are a dying breed and never were big spenders."

Den, always brimming with ideas, suggested, "Why not a Tony's Biker Bar?"

Tony seemed to consider the name before responding. "I think about menu composition and new recipe ideas a lot while riding. And I notice how food affects my time on the saddle." He held up a bun. "Consider a cinnamon roll. Its size, sweetness, ingredients–all crafted to be indulgent without disruption. They're not health food—but they're not crap like most, either. You can eat a Tony's pastry or two and ride happy."

My mind reeled. Not only was Tony's gooey concoction super delicious, I could eat two and not feel ill, get the trots, or otherwise be compromised while riding. "You, sir, are a culinary wizard!"

Tony gave credit where it was due. "My secret ingredient... Elena. She's the one with the patience to fiddle and adjust."

"There should be a list of what to eat when riding," Earl proposed.

Like building a chopper, cafe racer, or a rat bike, we each had our own food likes and dislikes. Den, for example, relishes shredded baked Brussel sprouts.

There was unanimous agreement on one important point: food can significantly affect travel enjoyment and impact situational awareness.

"We can't ride on celery sticks alone."

"Or beer instead of water."

"Bikers love to stop for tasty snacks."

Food and drink, it seemed, are like fuel for your bike—the choice between sludge or rocket fuel can make or break a ride. And, like in any group, we each had our own road trip food stories to share. Delicious discoveries. What to avoid. Best snacks to carry. That sort of wisdom.

Food for Thought

As the conversation meandered through various food topics, SQUID Dolores offered a suggestion, "Go all the way? Full vegan?"

Marta added to the whimsical idea, "The Vegan Riders Cafe."

"Is there such a thing as an outlaw who doesn't eat cheese?" Conrad asked?

"Cut out dairy last year," Earl announced. "Doctor's orders. "But not curves."

"Like Victorys, there aren't many vegan riders," Tony said.

"They crave meat and become Indians," I said.

"I own lean mean machines," Manny said. "Like my body."

As the conversation wound down, Den glanced at the clock and said, "Elena, could I get a meat lovers panini? Lunchtime. "

"Coming right up," Elena answered with a warm smile. She has a sweet spot for Den.

Den added, "Before you lop it off your menu."

"We can always make one for you, Denis."

Not wanting to be left out, I placed my order. "I'll just have a cinnamon roll, please Elena, when you have time."

"I'm starving," Conrad said. "Elena, any of last month's Tart of the Months left?"

Manny raised his coffee. "To food and flow."

22

List 18: Helmeted Emotions

And Other Internal Combustions

> "Emotions can get in the way or get you on the way."
> Mavis Mazhura.

Manny confessed, "Didn't sleep much. Rat bike drama. Family stuff. I'm emotionally wiped."

Marta opened an article titled "How To Deal With Emotions in a Healthy Way."

"Skip it," Earl said. "The answer's obvious—ride."

But Manny's bike was parked for the Dark Season. Nevertheless, the gang responded with their usual banter:

"Pull a wheelie.

"Hit the trail, Jack."

"Lean hard."

"Scrape your pegs."

"Follow the Yellow Brick Road."

Marta, undeterred by our antics, began reading excerpts from the article aloud. It was immediately clear that the advice didn't resonate at all. There was a collective sense that, for us, riding is more than just a means of escaping emotional turmoil; it's a way of life and the expert hadn't reached that level.

"Not so fast," Manny said. "My bike isn't insured. Wind therapy isn't an option. What do you do when you can't ride?" He'd confessed to being 'emotionally depleted' due to a family matter, not just the rat bike.

"Want to borrow mine?" Cam asked thoughtfully, confident his offer would be rejected.

"Fresh savory buns on the house?" Tony didn't wait for an answer; he gave Elena the signal.

Not shying away, Dolores teased, "You don't look depleted, tough guy." Her light-hearted comment opened the floor to a broader conversation about emotions. Are outlaws as resilient and tough as they portray themselves to be? Do bikers have normal, mainstream emotions?

Marta suggested, "We are human, beneath our gear and under our helmets."

At that moment, Elena arrived carrying a tray of buns fresh from the oven.

She balanced the tray with the elegance of a rider leaning into a sweeper." Very professional, I thought..

Manny took a bite. "Let's make a list," he said. We knew exactly where to start.

Our List of Biker Emotional Clues

Melancholy: Neglected bikes wear it like a tarp—frayed, forgotten. Hopefully, you don't spot your old bike, left to rot by someone who swore they'd cherish her.

Heartbreak: Your once-faithful ride won't start. "We've grown apart," she whispers.

Euphoria: Your bike sputters out—but miraculously coasts to a gas pump. Then you spot a sign: wings on special. You do a little gas dance.

LIST 18: HELMETED EMOTIONS

Shock: You dismount, hear an odd sound. Is it your engine? No. It slithers. A rattlesnake—welded to the ground, the unholy opposite of 'the wheels are round and they roll.'

Relief: You're hopelessly stuck up Shit Creek, stranded, deflated, and out of ideas. Then Motorcycle MAGIC happens—a group of classic bikers pulls in.

Pissed Off: Rain's coming. You could beat it—if only you could find your damn pannier key.

Obsessive: Too many oil changes, wax jobs, and one preload adjustment too many.

Competitive: You're obsessed with setting a new record, shattering your GPS's predicted arrival time.

Bored: If I was in a car, I could nap.

Sickly: A mile down the road, the gas station hot dog has your stomach turning like a radiator fan.

Terror: Cresting a hill, antlers. A semi. Your life—flashing by as a hood ornament.

Disgust: As you're walking away from your polished beauty at a meet-up, your eyes fall on a missed spot the size of a black hole.

Awe: Mother Nature puts on a show reserved for motorcycles only.

Hostility: It was a nice day until the cop fired his rule book at you and tossed in an insincere 'Bikers' Lives Matter' lecture. '

Quirky: The wind makes you laugh for no reason.

Nostalgia: A glimpse of your first bike passing by. Suddenly, you're a SQUID again.

Motorcycle JOY: You know JOY when it comes, but it can't be described.

Tranquil: You've arrived on the Road to JOY—all of your mental trash is gone.

Desperation: The Ass Problem escalates. Diarrhea joins the ride.

Workplace Anger: Bosses or clients who make you wish you were riding. Taking a walking break isn't enough.

Humility: Those who proudly ride humble bikes are exalted.

Manny pointed at his bun. "Love it, Tony. It's put me in the mood to visit the dealership. To check out the new arrivals."

We'd all seen posts enticing us to come on in and buy one of the sparkling new beauties. They promised to be better than ever. Nothing soothes a soul like cinnamon and shiny chrome. Shopping for a bike can cure feeling emotionally depleted.

Manny extended an invitation, asking, "Anyone want to come along?"

In a show of solidarity, everyone at the table rose.

Marta hesitated. "But they don't sell Guzzis."

Solidarity comes first. Helmets on. One of us was feeling down—and we ride toward restoration.

.

23

◈ Waypoint 4: The Endless Highway

Fuel, flow, and rhythm—on the road and within.
The Road to Joy continues. Just turn the page.

24

List 19: Fuel for Thought

"The price of gas is going up again."

"EV," I said. "No worries on that front."

Cam met my indifference with a nod. "Motorcycle. Not bothered."

"Cafes are like gas stations," Tony said. "Pull in, refuel—body or bike—and move on."

"Or just pop in for a pit stop. Take a leak and you're off."

Tony frowned.

"At least buy a snack," Marta insisted.

"The need for gas forces you to stop. Take a rest break. It's a good thing," Conrad said.

"If you rode an electric bike, you could nap while it charges," I added.

"Or read *War and Peace*," Dolores joked. "Charging stations could double as libraries."

"They're great meetup spots," Den said. "They'll be missed if they disappear."

Tony swirled his coffee, then nodded. "Even gas station coffee has evolved."

Marta, steering the conversation, brought us back on track. "Sounds like we've got a list of gas station memories."

"They sound like weird shrines," SQUID Dolores said. "Full of miracles and failures."

Some Of Our Gas Station Moments

Pleasant Memories

• Your group rolls in and there's a pump for every bike and a bike for every pump.

• In addition to being incredibly friendly, the clerk is also an avid rider and gladly divulges the location of a secret road. Want to meet up sometime, honey?

• Grinning while cagers watch their gas bill spin up.

• Bug goo be gone! Fresh water, a working squeegee, and a full roll of paper towels at your pump.

• Of the six bikes at the station, a Motorcycle Dreamer tells you he loves your bike best.

• Thank god for your buddy's tiny gas tank. It gave you time to deal discreetly with the Ass Problem.

• The greasy food was sold out—spared from throwing a rod down the road.

• Is that Marilyn Monroe at the next pump? Look at her, lusting after my machine. Want to meet up down the road, honey?

• The pump's color scheme sets off your bike like gallery lighting. You pause, snap a pic, and feel a swell of pride.

• Just as you're ready to leave, a traffic light halts the incessant Road Vomit, clearing the way for you to throttle up and escape.

• You look over and see the biker at the next pump is the guy you never got along with in high school. Your bike wins the day

• You top off your tank just as the price jumps twenty cents. For once, you beat the algorithm.

• Some stops are just gas. Others fine-tune your Motorcycle State of Mind.

"More truths hit mid-ride," than at the pumps," Earl said.

"Or when you're stuck at a red light," Tony said.

"With a half a Snickers bar, the one you bought at the gas station, melting in your jacket pocket," Conrad said.

Infuriating Moments

• While waiting your turn in line to pay for the drink you unfortunately opened, the cager at the front fumbles for change, then drops coins on the floor.

• Welcome to One Pump Town. No one's minding the store.

• The road sign pointing to gas turned out to be a lie. The station was in the next county.

• Fumbling with the air compressor you paid to use causes your tire to lose even more pressure. Then you see the out-of-order sign.

• The obese cager ahead of you didn't flush fully.

• The attendant hates his job and doesn't know which direction is west.

• As you flush, a sinking realization hits—your keys fell into the toilet bowl.

• Pay at the pump works for the cagers, but not at your pump. Sometimes it's hard to ignore conspiracy theories.

- LIST 19: FUEL FOR THOUGHT

• The fumes smell like diesel.

Cam tossed his napkin onto the table. "Nothing like a good gas stop to remind you why we ride."
Marta nodded. "Or why I carry wet wipes."
As the conversation lulled, I seized the moment. "Can I offer a motorcycle gas joke?" I didn't wait for permission. "My bike was doing 110 when a cop pulled me over. He asked, 'Why so fast?' I said, 'Because I twisted the throttle, which made more fuel go to the engine.'"
Thanks, Steven Wright.
Marta added, "My EV charges in silence—no fumes, no mess. But it's never led me to a biker with a secret road."

25

All Lists Must End

Two days before the grand reopening, Tony remained remarkably calm. Elena, however, resembled a squirming SQUID on her maiden voyage—torn between taming the machine, mastering the road, and testing her mettle. Tony, sensing Elena's stress, offered his usual blend of advice and humor: "Lean hard and accelerate out, Elena. And remember to check the fruit salad."

We were gathered around two new tables for the 'soft opening.' Each of us ordered a different item from the new list, and, after tasting, unanimously declared all the food items as well as the coffees to be fantastic.

Cam arrived late, decked out in his summer jacket. "Beautiful day." The Dark Season had released its grip on the land. Outside:

Birds were learning to sing.

Oil warmed.

Trails dried.

Grass flourished.

Nature rebalanced.

Insurance policies were renewing.

Machines grew restless.

Riders itched.

Cam appeared reborn, and a magical vitality hung over the bistro. "Are we ready for the Tony's celebration ride?"

"Can't wait," Manny replied, his excitement evident. He'd purchased a new machine and so no longer felt emotionally depleted.

Conrad wore his amber tee shirt, the colour of JOY.

"All set." Tony picked his helmet up. "Let's go!" Turning to Elena he added, "Back by three."

Having long since abandoned any hope of focusing her boss solely on business, Elena gave a halfhearted nod of disapproval. For his part, Tony no longer bothered to explain, "My motorcycle is an extension of the workspace, Elena. It's where my best ideas are born."

Due to the grand reopening being so close, Elena found the business disregard to be completely inexcusable. The constant joy riding would soon be at odds with baking and management. Excuses like 'I need to tune my state of mind' or 'I must empty my mental trash,' she found bewildering. Nevertheless, the assistant manager called, "Keep the rubber side down." May your travels be flat as a pancake and slow as molasses.

With the fading roar of engines in the background, Elena withdrew a notepad from her apron pocket. The heading on the first page read, **'Very Important To-Dos.'** She scanned the list as if it were a treasure map—hoping, perhaps, it might lead her somewhere unexpected.

Then "Elena flipped the page and wrote:

1. Fruit salad.
2. Helmets back by three.
3. Maybe... try an ebike ... to start."

26

◈ Final Waypoint: Ride Your Route

No more waypoints on our map. The road ahead is yours.

Wherever it leads, may it be full throttle joy with stories worth repeating.

Ride On.

Have a list-worthy moment?
Drop us a line (post or message) Scraping Pegs on Facebook.

27

◈ Appendix A: Vocabulary You Didn't Know You Need

"The English language was born Before Motorcycle," Marta once claimed. "It struggles to capture the essence of the ride." She wasn't wrong. Riders once relied on hand signals and silence—until Bluetooth headsets turned us all into chatty tour guides.

Over time, our crew developed a lingo all its own. You'll find these terms sprinkled throughout the *Scraping Pegs* books. They aren't just inside jokes—many are necessary to fill gaps in the English language.

Here's our unofficial, irreverent glossary. Study it. Share it. Add your own.

After Motorcycle (AM)
The era that began with the invention of the motorcycle in 1885. Coined by Marta, this marks the age of true progress—post-shovel, post-pottery, post-horseshit.

Anticipation JOY
The elation before a ride. Often involves humming, dancing, fidgeting, polishing chrome, or counting sleeps like a kid before Christmas.

APPENDIX A: VOCABULARY YOU DIDN'T KNOW YOU NEED

The Ass Problem
That seat + butt mismatch that feels like rusty daggers dipped in fire ants. No known cure (though your family upholsterer may provide some relief).

Before Motorcycle (BM)
Aka pre-civilization. Archaeologists missed the point. There are only two eras: Before Motorcycle and After Motorcycle.

Blockheads
Riders who look competent but ride like they learned from TikTok. Trapped forever in the 'Born to be wild, don't tell me how to ride,' phase.

Blockhead Moment
That lapse when you forget you're not Valentino Rossi. Happens to us all.

Cagers
Drivers of four-wheeled vehicles, safely cocooned and often unaware of our existence.

Cager Saints
Rare cagers who drive respectfully and don't try to kill us. Salute them.

Complacency Swamp
The mental fog that sneaks up during long, straight rides. Usually found near Nothingness Highway.

Constant Walker
A crash survivor's milestone. Past the cane, past the limp—toward the really big goal: riding again.

The Dark Season
That dark, cold time when bikes hibernate and riders go slightly mad.

APPENDIX A: VOCABULARY YOU DIDN'T KNOW YOU NEED

Disconnectedness
That floaty, calm, in-the-zone feeling you get while riding. Cannot be achieved in cars, cubicles, or yoga class.

Emergency Ass Pullover
When your butt taps out mid-ride. May require a roadside hand rub or guardrail massage.

Farkles
Shiny accessories you don't need but must have. Includes sissy bars, tail bags, and bells.

Freedomites
Helmetless warriors who risk it all for freedom. May your rubber side always stay down.

The Gas Station Assumption
Blind faith leading you to believe fuel is just around the bend. It never is.

Gotta Go
The itch. The urge. The need to ride, often without a clear destination.

The Great Motorcycle Debate
Are two wheels mandatory? Do trikes have one wheel too many? Scooters?

Half-Biker
A term snobs use to describe anyone not riding *their* way. Ignore them.

Horace the Horrible
The beast that leaps in front of your bike at the worst time. Can bring your number up in the Motorcycle Lottery.

APPENDIX A: VOCABULARY YOU DIDN'T KNOW YOU NEED

Hunker Down & Grind It Out
A technique for surviving long, boring roads. Engage grit mode.

Insensitive Assholes
Riders blessed with perfect butt-to-seat ratios. We envy them.

It'll Do Bikes
The bike you have while dreaming of your next one. It gets the job done.

JOY
See: *The Joy of Motorcycles*. It's the opposite of Motorcycle Misery.

Killer Bikes
Or just ones you should've serviced 2,000 miles ago.

Loner-By-Choice
The solo rider who thrives alone. Often wise. Sometimes weird.

Loud Pipe–Loud Music Lovers (LPLMs)
Pipes at full blast. Music at full blast. Tinnitus as lifestyle choice. Hard to ignore.

Motorcycle Allowance
The reasonable policy that should exist—but doesn't—that favors two wheels in all things.

Motorcycle Cunts
Loud, arrogant, intrusive, and usually reckless. Doesn't matter the bike, brand, outfit, or gender.

Motorcycle Dreamer
Talks about buying a bike. Never pulls the trigger. Often nearby, admiring your ride.

Motorcycle Friends
Bonded by bikes, not by resumes. The real ones.

APPENDIX A: VOCABULARY YOU DIDN'T KNOW YOU NEED

Motorcycle Lottery
"It's not if, it's when." One day, your number will come up.

Motorcycle Misery
When things go sideways. Usually precedes a good story.

Motorcycle Misery Tales
The wild rides you don't want to repeat but always tell.

Motorcycle Narcissism
That feeling when you know everyone is looking—and you want them to.

Motorcycle Neuromodulation
Scientific term for the brain chemicals bikes are known to release. No prescription needed.

Motorcycle Roulette
Taking dumb risks, betting you'll make it… probably.

The Motorcycle Wave Dilemma
Do you wave first? Do you wave back? Do scooters count? Existential crisis on two wheels.

Motorcycle Yin-Yang
Two wheels. One soul. All things in balance—until they're not.

NimRods
Those who don't get it. Like, at all.

Nothingness Highway
The long, straight stretch through landscape that makes you question existence.

APPENDIX A: VOCABULARY YOU DIDN'T KNOW YOU NEED

Oddballs
The gear's old, the bike's louder than it should be, but the heart's in the right place.

Road Vomit
Gridlock hell. Where throttle dies, joy evaporates, and exhaust fills your lungs. The place motorcycle souls go to die.

SQUID
Young, brash, reckless. Think bullet bike and no gloves.

Transport Bike
You ride it to work, to school, to your mom's. Not for fun. Sad, but sometimes necessary.

The Teddy Bear Theory
Sometimes, a motorcycle is the only thing that makes you feel better.

28

Afterword

Thanks for adding a bullet on the motorcycle reading list!
Leave a comment. Send a message. Get book updates.
Scraping Pegs on Facebook.

BOOKS BY THE AUTHOR

Scraping Pegs, The Truth About Motorcycles

The Joy of Motorcycles, More Scraping Pegs

Scrape Your Lists, The Motorcycle Files

Motorcycle State of Mind, Beyond Scraping Pegs

The Motorcycle Prescription, Scrape Your Therapy

Book Information: Scraping Pegs on Facebook

www.ingramcontent.com/pod-product-compliance
Lightning Source LLC
Chambersburg PA
CBHW072101110526
44590CB00018B/3265